Killarney National Park

A Place to Treasure

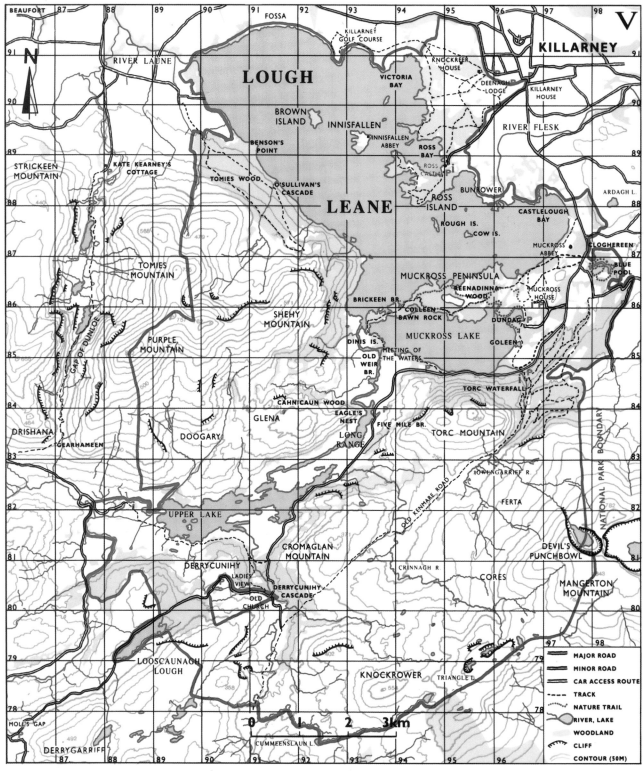

BASED ON THE ORDNANCE SURVEY OF IRELAND BY PERMISSION OF THE GOVERNMENT (PERMIT NO 6043)

KILLARNEY NATIONAL PARK
A Place to Treasure

Edited by
Bill Quirke

The Collins Press

Published in 2001 by
The Collins Press,
West Link Park,
Doughcloyne,
Wilton,
Cork

British Library Cataloguing in Publication data.

Typesetting by Red Barn Publishing

Jacket design by Jackie Raftery

ISBN: 1-898256-69-1

The views expressed in this book are those of the individual writers, and are not necessarily shared by the editor, the other chapter authors, or by Dúchas – The Heritage Service.
The editing and writing of this book was without renumeration.
All royalties from the sales of the book will go to Groundwork Conservation Volunteers, who by their work every summer since 1981 have held out the possibility of a long-term future for more than a quarter of the native oakwoods of the National Park. The Groundwork Killarney project is the largest voluntary nature conservation project in the history of the state and has from its inception been generously supported and encouraged by the National Parks Service.

Printed in Spain by E.G. ZURE (E-48950 Erandio)

Contents

Acknowledgements

The chapter authors listed at the end of this book have given of their knowledge, expertise and love of the national park without any recompense. All writing and editing for this book has been voluntary. Photographs and other illustrations have also been made available free of charge by Seán Ryan, Daniel Kelly, Pascal Sweeney, William O'Brien, Padraig O'Donoghue, Paudie O'Leary, John Earley, Bill Quirke, The Department of Irish Folklore, University College Dublin and Dúchas – The Heritage Service and the National Museum of Ireland.

Various sections of the text were read and/or helpful suggestions for improvements made by Alan Craig, Helena Twomey, Kathy Quirke, Marjorie and Michael Quirke, Jimi Conroy, Pascal Sweeney, Kathryn Freeman, Paudie O'Leary, Peter O'Toole, John O'Connor, Pascal Dower, Tim Burkitt, Padraig O'Sullivan, Jim Larner, Coilín MacLochlainn, Brendan O'Shea Chris Smal, and Daniel Kelly; their contribution to this book has been large. However, any errors in the editing of the book are solely mine.

In addition to the research carried out by the authors, this book draws on the findings of other researchers, including Niall Ó Maoiléidigh, Áine Ní Shuilleabháin, Aileen O'Sullivan, Fraser Mitchell, Martin O'Grady, Peter O'Toole, James O'Connor, and Chris Smal. Their contribution to our knowledge of Killarney national park is warmly acknowledged.

I am grateful to Dúchas – the Heritage Service for agreeing in advance of publication to purchase a substantial number of copies of this book for sale at its outlets.

Finally, I want to thank Richard Bradshaw who did so much work in the early stages of this book. Richard's involvement was ended by his move to Sweden, but without him this book would never have been produced.

Chapter 1

KILLARNEY NATIONAL PARK – AN INTRODUCTION

Alan J. Craig

Killarney National Park owes its existence as a national park to the remark-able generosity of Senator Arthur Vincent and his parents-in-law, Mr and Mrs William Bowers Bourn. In 1932, they gave the 4,300-hectare Muckross Estate to the people of Ireland, to be managed as a national park, called the Bourn Vincent Memorial Park in memory of Senator Vincent's wife, Maud, who had died a few years earlier. On 1 January 1933, following the passage of the Bourn Vincent Memorial Park Act, the Commissioners of Public Works became responsible for the management of the new national park.

There had been public parks in state ownership in Ireland for many years, such as Phoenix Park and Saint Stephen's Green in Dublin. But the term national park was new to Ireland, although presumably well known to the donors, who would have been familiar with Yellowstone and other famous examples in America, where the concept had originated. In the early years of the new national park there was little positive management of it for conser-vation or for recreational use. The demesne lands beside the lakes were open to the public, as they had been when in private ownership, but the estate as a whole was managed primarily as an extensive farm. This remained the case until the 1960s when, in a period of economic and social change, various new proposals were made for use of park lands and buildings, including intensive experimental sheep-farming by the Agricultural Research Institute. Fears were expressed about the future of the park, and particularly the survival of the red deer herd. For the first time since 1932, politicians and civil servants respon-sible for the park gave serious consideration to its role. They looked to other countries to see how they managed their national parks. Two of their decisions arising from this international review had far-reaching effects on the future of the Bourn Vincent Memorial Park. Firstly, they decided that the internation-al criteria and standards for national parks which had been developed with

Senator Arthur Vincent who with his parents-in-law, Mr and Mrs Bowers Bourn, presented the original Bourn Vincent Memorial Park to the State in 1932. (Dúchas)

United Nations approval by I.U.C.N., now known as the World Conservation Union, should be applied in Ireland. Secondly, they decided that the national park at Killarney should be extended, if the opportunity arose, to make it more effective. Property acquisitions between 1972 and 1996 created a continuous tract of national park, more than doubling the size to 10,289 hectares (25,400 acres). The extended national park, incorporating the Bourn Vincent Memorial Park, is referred to as Killarney National Park.

National parks vary considerably in different countries, but common to most of them are two basic purposes, to protect and conserve nature and landscape and to provide for public enjoyment. This has been expressed in legislation and policy statements from the 1916 Act, which established the U.S. National Parks Service, onwards. It has been generally recognised that the two purposes can be in conflict and that if they are, conservation must prevail. For Irish purposes a working definition has been formulated which takes account of this problem: 'National Parks exist to conserve natural plant and animal communities and scenic landscapes which are both extensive and of national importance, and under conditions compatible with that purpose, to enable people to visit and appreciate them.'

The first objective of Killarney National Park, therefore, is nature conservation. The ecosystems and natural features of Killarney are rated by ecologists as being of international significance, so there is much to conserve. Such considerations hardly influenced the former owners of the Muckross estate when they decided that it should become a national park. Yet it can safely be said that even without their generosity and foresight, the area would have become one of the first choices, on scientific grounds, for protection as a national park, some 30 or 40 years later.

The most extensive remaining areas of natural or semi-natural woodland in Ireland are found around Killarney, almost all now within the national park. Most of these woods are dominated by oak, with much birch and an understorey of holly. On limestone pavement between Lough Leane and Muckross Lake there is a unique yew wood, and there are extensive wet woodlands, mostly dominated by alder. All the woodlands are strongly oceanic, with abundant mosses, liverworts and filmy ferns on the ground and on the trees themselves, favoured by the mild, moist climate. The greater part of the park is covered by low-growing blanket bog and wet heath vegetation, not very unusual in Ireland but rare internationally. Red deer inhabiting the national park are the only indigenous wild herd of deer remaining in the country. The lakes and rivers are also a rich wildlife habitat, with two unusual kinds of fish and many rare invertebrates. Several plants more usually found in southern and south-western Europe are frequent in the park, most notably the arbutus or strawberry tree.

Conserving nature in the park does not always mean leaving it alone. Active management is often necessary, usually in response to past human disturbance. Much effort has been devoted to countering the spread of *Rhododendron ponticum*, widely planted during the last century, which has had a devastating effect on the oakwoods. The fight to clear existing infestation and prevent further spread will have to continue for many years. Large numbers of sika deer, also an introduced species, have been culled in the hope of achieving a healthier balance between grazing animals and their habitat. In other cases, just leaving wildlife alone can achieve a great deal. Red deer numbers have been enabled to increase from alarmingly low levels 30 years ago by a policy of strict protection from harmful impacts. Ultimately though, deliberate control of red deer numbers will become necessary in the absence of wolves and other natural predators of earlier times. The general approach is to encourage the fullest possible operation of natural processes and to minimise the effects of human interference.

The second fundamental objective of Killarney National Park is to provide for public appreciation of the natural heritage within the park. This has been achieved by a variety of facilities and services for visitors which go under the general name of interpretation. Interpretation has been described as 'a painless form of education aimed at the casual visitor'.

There are self-guiding nature trails in the park, with numbered stops and illustrated booklets to explain their features. Another trail, geared to the needs of the visually handicapped, focuses on the sounds, smells and textures of nature, and has a guide-rope and a recorded commentary on cassette. The

Muckross Abbey. (Dúchas)

principal park visitor centre in a wing of Muckross House includes an audio-visual introduction to the national park, and an exhibition featuring the oak-woods of Killarney. There are smaller displays in other information offices within the park. Park publications include a general booklet describing the main features of the park and suggesting places to visit, a detailed map jointly published with the Ordnance Survey and a growing range of illustrated booklets on specific aspects of the park's heritage. Each autumn a series of illustrated talks on topics related to the park is well attended by local people.

Such interpretative programmes are not the only way by which appreciation of the natural heritage of the park is developed. Many visitors never avail of these specific facilities but come to appreciate the park and its qualities through its many informal recreational opportunities including walking, cycling, jaunting-car and boat trips, or simply sitting admiring the scenery and enjoying the tranquillity of their surroundings. On the other hand, others find out about it through formal education by attending field courses, or by participating as volunteers in conservation work projects.

Innisfallen Oratory.
(Dúchas)

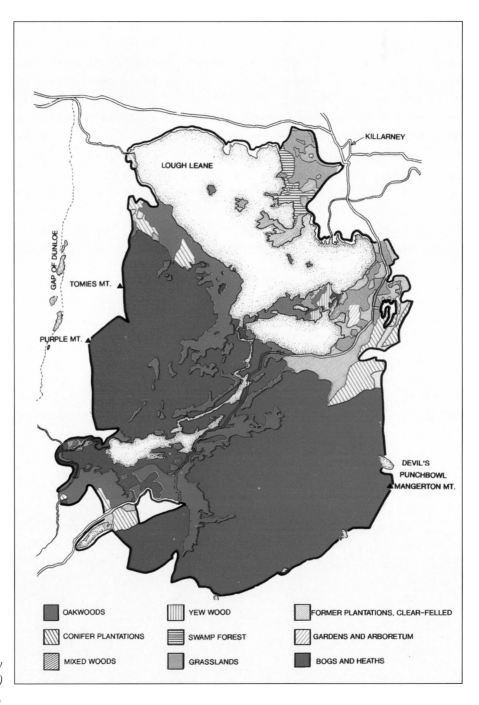

*Habitat map of Killarney
National Park. (Dúchas)*

The two essential purposes of a national park do not preclude it from achieving other desirable objectives. For Killarney National Park one such objective is to conserve features of historic and cultural interest within the park. Landscaped demesnes were laid out in the eighteenth and nineteenth centuries within the great estates. Antiquities incorporated in these demesnes included the remains of an early Christian monastery on the island of Inisfallen, the fifteenth-century Franciscan Friary church known as Muckross Abbey, and the beautifully located medieval tower house known as Ross Castle. To the existing features, natural and man-made, the landscapers added lawns and parkland scattered with trees, avenues and vistas, and picturesque bridges, boathouses and lodges. Muckross House, a nineteenth-century mansion, has its principal rooms furnished in period style, but also houses a museum of Kerry folklife, managed by local trustees in co-operation with the park authorities. The Trustees' folklife activities have been extended to lands near the house, where traditional farming practices are demonstrated. Beside the house are fine gardens noted particularly for their rhododendrons and azaleas and for their informal lawns in a woodland setting.

The national park also has a valuable role as a place where environmental research and monitoring can be carried on under relatively natural conditions. The national park authorities have supported a substantial and wide-ranging programme of scientific research over the last 30 years mainly carried out by the staff and postgraduate students of Irish universities. Major topics of research have included the ecology of red deer and other mammals, description of woodland and moorland plant communities, ecology and eutrophication studies in the lakes, vegetation history including the effects of fire, the impacts of introduced species such as rhododendron and sika deer, the potential benefits to upland habitats from re-introduction of Kerry cattle, and surveys of bird communities. All this research has provided useful information for the management of the park and for publication in scientific papers and more popular literature, including this book. The importance of the park for research has been reinforced by its designation by UNESCO as one of a global network of Biosphere Reserves.

A national park cannot flourish in isolation. It is important that it should function in harmony with the local community, and that changes in the surrounding area should not threaten its integrity. The development of Killarney town has been based largely on tourism, the area having attracted visitors for over 200 years. It is therefore very important for the local community that the park should continue to protect many of the natural assets that attract tourists to Killarney. The extent of local interest in the park has been demonstrated in many ways, ranging from large attendances on special occasions to campaigns and media coverage during controversies affecting the park.

Policies for the park must recognise its significance to the community, while local developments need to take account of impacts on the park with its internationally significant features. In some countries formal zoning and consultation procedures have been established to reconcile conservation with development in and around national parks. Similar systems may be of use in Killarney in the future.

The park now has the benefit of a published management plan, setting out its objectives, outlining the policies to be pursued to achieve them, and defining zoning within the park to balance the various objectives satisfactorily. This has provided a sound basis on which to build increased public support for the park and its objectives. There is now also a good prospect of new legislation to provide more secure protection for all Irish national parks, including Killarney National Park which led the way for the other parks established in recent years.

Chapter 2

THE MAKING OF THE LANDSCAPE

Richard Thorn and Peter Coxon

The longest and most extraordinary story of Killarney National Park is the story of the shape and substance of the landscape itself. In this story 'impossibilities' become commonplace. The story tells how this piece of the earth's surface that is now Killarney National Park was not always here but was in many different other places, sometimes many thousands of miles away in an entirely different part of the globe; it tells how the high peaks that dominate the park landscape were once the bed of a primeval lake basin; it tells how the rocks you can now walk upon were once many hundreds of metres underground; it tells how the substance of the rock you can pick up on the lake shore was once alive, swimming, crawling and growing in a tropical ocean.

The basic 'stuff' of the Killarney landscape is rock; rock clothed in soil, in water and in vegetation. Before we can describe how this basic rock was sculpted into its present shape we must examine the raw material itself. The final product of a human sculptor will depend greatly on the raw material with which he works; type of wood; type of metal; type of stone. The final product of the great forces that have shaped the landscape of Killarney has been greatly influenced by the nature of the raw materials on which they have worked – the different rock types that form the landscape.

The Making of the Rock (before 290 million years ago)

To recount how the raw materials of the Killarney landscape came into being we must travel back over unimaginable reaches of time, back over 400 million years. Geologists now accept that the great continents of the earth are actually vast solid plates of rock which 'float' on the less solid layers of rock below. Over periods measured in millions of years these 'tectonic plates' have literally drifted around the surface of the planet, sometimes separating from each other, sometimes colliding and throwing up great mountain chains.

Let us imagine ourselves as passengers of a satellite orbiting the earth 400 million years ago seeking the piece of the earth's crust that is now the south of Ireland and Killarney National Park. We would seek in vain in the northern latitudes where Ireland now lies. To succeed we would have to direct our orbit well to the south of the equator. We would find the 'embryonic' Ireland and the 'embryonic' Killarney landscape as part of a large continental mass consisting of Northern Europe and North America. This land mass, known as the Old Red Continent, lay between the equator and 30 degrees south, as far south as Brisbane and Durban are today. The climate was hot and frequently arid. Rainfall, when it occurred, was torrential and caused rapid erosion of the rugged highlands to the north, which included the mountains of Connemara, Wicklow and Donegal as well as the mountains of Scandinavia, Scotland and Newfoundland. Rivers flowing southwards from these mountains traversed an alluvial plain bounded by wide bays of sand and mud to the south of Cork and Kerry, before flowing into the ocean. In the Kerry area, sediments eroded from the highlands were deposited in a large land-locked basin. Geologists call this the South Munster Basin and its deepest part was along a line running from the Iveragh Peninsula (the Ring of Kerry) into County Cork.

The eroded particles washed from the mountains of the Old Red Continent into the South Munster Basin were of the hard and durable mineral called quartz. We are all familiar with how particles deposited by water on beaches or in rivers or lakes, can vary from fine mud and silt, to various grades of sand, up to gravel and small stones, depending on conditions. Conditions in the South Munster Basin varied. In quiet pools and lakes away from the main areas of sediment accumulation, small mud-sized particles were deposited. Close to inflowing rivers, which had sufficient velocity and turbulence to carry much larger particles, coarse sand and gravels were deposited. In intermediate conditions sand was deposited. This period of sedimentation lasted about five million years and is called the Devonian period by geologists. The different grades of sediment became compacted and transformed into different types of rock: the fine sediments forming the shales; the sand sediments forming the sandstones that are so plentiful in the

The sandstone of the Killarney area was deposited in the 'South Munster Basin' 400 to 345 million years ago. The ripple pattern of the shallow water in which it was deposited shows clearly on this rock face in the Macgillycuddys Reeks. (Seán Ryan)

park and the coarser sediments forming what are called conglomerates. Most of Killarney National Park and much of County Kerry is composed of rocks deposited in the South Munster Basin during this period.

Some volcanic rock in the park also dates from this period. A volcanic rock is formed when, as a result of the movement of the tectonic plates, molten rock from the earth's mantle is ejected on to the surface and solidifies. An example of one type of volcanic rock, called felsite, which was ejected as ash during this period, is visible in the cliffs overlooking the Devil's Punchbowl on the northern side of Mangerton. Pieces of the rock, which is pale grey in colour with whitish, irregular shaped fragments in it, can be found on the path just below the Devil's Punchbowl.

By the end of the Devonian period, about 345 million years ago, the rugged highlands of the north had been greatly diminished in stature by unrelenting weathering and erosion. About this time, perhaps due to the shifting of tectonic plates to the south, the sea, which for so long had bordered the southern edge of the Old Red Continent, began to slowly advance northwards over the land, forming a warm shallow sea like parts of the Caribbean today.

The period that geologists call the Carboniferous Period had begun. The influx of the sea resulted in a change in the type of sediments which were deposited. Whereas the sediments derived from the land had been mostly sandstones and conglomerates, those deposited in the ocean during the early part of the marine influx were mainly mudstones (derived from very fine particles) and shales, with fewer sandstones. Because of its low lying position, the South Munster Basin was first to be flooded. The initial stage of this marine influx can be clearly seen at Brickeen bridge on the Muckross Peninsula (Grid Ref. V938858). As the waters of the ocean deepened and rose over the land, the type of rock that was formed changed. Instead of shales and mudstones, limestone became the predominant rock type. Limestone, which is composed principally of calcium carbonate, is derived from two sources: firstly, by precipitation of lime from sea water, and secondly, by accumulation on the ocean floor of fragments of stems and shells of animals which had used calcium carbonate in the formation of these hard parts. At this time the ocean was warm as it lay just to the north of the equator.

Further advances and retreats of the ocean deposited further layers of sedimentary rock. But once the layers of limestone had been deposited over the earlier sandstone, the principal raw materials of the Killarney landscape had been formed and sealed beneath layers of younger sediments all of which still lay beneath the ocean. Once the raw materials had been formed, the great sculpting, which continues to the present day, began.

The Sculpting of the Landscape (290 to 65 million years ago)

About 290 million years ago the northward moving tectonic plate carrying the continent of Africa collided with the plate carrying Ireland and Europe. This collision caused a tremendous buckling and cracking of the colliding plates. In Cork and Kerry the layers of sedimented rock that had formed beneath the ocean were folded and faulted on a massive scale, raising them above the ocean into high mountains. Because the thrust of the colliding plates was from the south, the axis of folding runs in an east-west direction. And this pattern can still be clearly seen on a map of south-west Ireland. Faulting is the process whereby rock strata shear under pressure and then move vertically or horizontally relative to one another. In this way older rocks can come to stand high above younger rock formations in the landscape. Evidence of one of the most important faults caused by this mountain building episode is clear to see in Killarney National Park. If you travel to Killarney by train, after Millstreet, a wall of mountains is visible to the south, leading towards the national park and ending in the north scarp face of Torc mountain. This is the Muckross-Millstreet fault. The rocks to the south of this fault, sandstone with overlying limestone and younger rock layers, were raised by as much as 3,000 metres relative to the rock layers to the north. These mountains towered three times higher than Mangerton. From Waterford through to Dingle Bay there is a clear boundary between highland and lowland, marked in places by fault lines such as the Muckross-Millstreet fault. Widespread erosion, which followed the formation of the mountains, stripped them of great thicknesses of Carboniferous rocks so that the underlying resistant Devonian rocks were exposed overlooking the Carboniferous limestone lowland to the north. This is still the situation today.

Another effect of faulting is to cause water in the rocks in the vicinity of the fault to become very hot and this allows metals which are dispersed in very low concentrations throughout the rock to melt and to be redeposited in concentrated lodes or veins. Copper veins at Muckross and Ross Island, mined since the Bronze Age, owe their existence to the presence nearby of the Muckross-Millstreet and other fault lines.

Between 345 and 300 million years ago the limestone of the Killarney area was deposited over the older sandstone. Long ago eroded from the mountains, it is the predominant rock type of the lowland areas of the national park. Around the lake shores the erosion of limestone continues, forming such striking features as Governor's rock on Ross Island. (Bill Quirke)

After the formation of the mountains, from 280 to 65 million years ago, many geological events took place of which no remaining trace can be found in the national park. The area which was to become Ireland continued to move over the earth's surface with the great slow drift of the tectonic plates. Erosion of the mountains continued and sea levels rose and fell. Most of Ireland was again submerged beneath the ocean and covered in a layer of chalk up to 100 metres thick, formed from the fine-grained sediment left by the calcareous shells of tiny planktonic organisms. Lava flows from volcanoes covered a large part of the country, burying it beneath great sheets of basalt rock. In the Killarney area, no rocks deposited during the whole of this period have been found. All were eroded away down to the old layers of sandstone and limestone of the present landscape.

The limestone caves of Muckross lake. (Seán Ryan)

The Tertiary Forests (65 to 2 million years ago)

We can assume that between 65 million and 2 million years ago, during the period called the Tertiary Period by geologists, the Killarney National Park area, like the rest of the country, was at first covered by dense forest and swamps, containing many tree species now extinct or found only in subtropical regions of the world. In conditions of high temperatures and monsoon-like rain there was rapid chemical alteration and weathering of the rock. Warm waters containing natural acids derived from the rich soil percolated down into the Carboniferous limestone forming caves and gorges, and weakened the sandstone to produce great thicknesses of rotted and chemically altered rock. Weathered rock was exposed in streams and river cuttings and

Limestone eroded into a complex and fantastic landscape with no covering of soil can be seen on the Muckross peninsula where the rocks are covered with blankets of moss and a rare woodland of yew trees. (Bill Quirke)

21

From Ladies View it is easy to see of how glacial ice flowing in a trough streamlines and smooths the land surface and widens and deepens its valley. Here the ice has eroded old red sandstone to form a deep wide valley containing glacially-scoured lakes. (Seán Ryan)

much was washed away during torrential rainstorms. The Killarney mountains were higher than they are now and were more rounded with river valleys carved into their heavily wooded slopes, and no sharp peaks on the skyline. The forests included monkey-puzzle trees, cypresses, palm trees and giant redwoods. We do not know if Lough Leane existed then; more probably the area at the foot of the mountains was an impenetrable lowland swamp similar to the Everglades of Florida today, with trees such as swamp cypress growing with their roots totally immersed in water. Within the swamps, intense solution of the limestone occurred and hollows so formed later enlarged to become a lake. Eventually the climate cooled as Ireland once again drifted northwards. The composition of the forests changed as warmth-loving species died out and were replaced by trees of more temperate latitudes.

Species such as pine, oak, elm, alder and hazel, all of which are familiar in Ireland today, covered the area. All this was to change as the climate deteriorated markedly and the great landscape sculpting forces of the ice age began to prevail.

Frost and Ice (2 million years ago to 10,000 years ago)

About 25 million years ago the world climate began to cool, and by two million years ago this had caused a rapid expansion of the polar ice caps. This last episode in geological time is known as the Quaternary or more commonly as the Ice Age. In this period polar waters have advanced southwards many times and ice sheets have built up on adjacent land masses. During these advances, the Gulf Stream was forced further to the south and cold polar currents washed Irish shores. All the mountain regions became centres of glacier growth and as the arctic conditions intensified, mountain glaciers coalesced as ice sheets spreading out over the lowlands. The earlier glaciations were the most extensive with ice sheets over 1,000 metres thick. However, arctic conditions were not continuous. Between the periods of glaciation, the average annual temperature reached and even exceeded that of today. For example, during the last interglacial period (120,000 years ago) hippopotamuses lived as far north as Leeds in Britain.

The landscape of Killarney National Park and the area around it has been greatly altered by the action of glacial ice and evidence of glacial erosion and deposition of eroded material covers the whole landscape. We know that glaciers have affected Killarney at least four times, but each successive glaciation has removed the evidence of the one that preceded it. This means that the most obvious effects are those of the last glaciation. This lasted from 115,000 to 10,000 years ago. We can reconstruct events prior to, and during, this ice advance from evidence collected in the Killarney area and around Ireland.

In the early days of the last glaciation, the Macgillycuddys Reeks were snow covered for long periods of the year, glistening in the weak sunshine after snow melt. The surrounding lowlands were a cold and desolate plain, with low vegetation of dwarf shrubs and grasses, similar to the northern regions of Siberia or Canada today. Lough Leane was frozen over for most of the year. Animals roaming the frozen landscape included wolf, stoat, brown bear, spotted hyena, Arctic hare, Arctic and Norway lemmings, woolly mammoth, reindeer and giant Irish deer. Fossil remains of all of these, dating from 34,000 years ago, were found in a cave in County Cork.

Temperatures were severe with large seasonal variations and daily ranges. The mean annual temperature was well below –8°C, compared with a present figure of 10°C for south-west Ireland. In the high summer, with the sun reaching the same position in the sky as it does today, the temperature may have risen to 15°C. In winter it would have fallen below –25°C, seldom exceeding freezing point even during the day. Temperatures on the mountain peaks would, of course, have been several degrees colder. Such variability in temperature, especially the daily variation, has a very important effect on rock structure. Imagine the Muckross Peninsula or even the peaks of the Macgillycuddys Reeks on a July or August day over 20,000 years ago. As the sun climbs in the sky, the frozen landscape slowly begins to thaw, and water is released to flow into cracks in the rocks. As night falls, so too does the temperature. Soon it is intensely cold and the water freezes. The water expands by 9 per cent when it freezes, with a force sufficient to break open solid rock along lines of weakness. This process, known as freeze-thaw action, occurred daily as the ice melted and then froze again. Such freeze-thaw action still occurs on the mountain peaks during winter today and the resulting shattered rocks can be seen near the summits. During the last glaciation, these processes occurred at all heights during the summer and also on warmer spring and autumn days – perhaps more than once a day for 100,000 years! The bleak landscape became covered in angular, shattered blocks of rock. The mountains of Old Red Sandstone were particularly affected and their surfaces were worn down and strewn with mantles of broken rock.

Around 25,000 years ago, temperatures fell still lower, probably as cold ocean currents from the Arctic swept further south and closer to Ireland. Cold, snow-laden winds blew from the Atlantic across Ireland. As the snow accumulated it gradually consolidated into enormous masses of ice, hundreds of metres thick. One ice cap developed between Antrim and Donegal, another in Galway and Roscommon and yet another in the southwest. Over hundreds of years, the ice thickened and produced ice sheets which spread under their own weight. The two northern ice caps coalesced to cover the northern and central parts of the country. The

Rock outcrops were smoothed by the ice into typical shapes known as roches moutonnées. (Seán Ryan)

south-west ice cap, centred west of Kenmare, remained isolated leaving an ice-free area in parts of Cork, Limerick and Kerry. Ice also accumulated on upland areas, including the Macgillycuddys Reeks, firstly as patches in the corries excavated during the previous glaciations and then as small mountain ice caps.

The Kenmare Ice Cap, and to a lesser extent the mountain ice in the Reeks, were critical in shaping the present-day scenery of Killarney National Park. The mountain ice excavated corries and deposited the small end moraines which lie outside them. Today many of these corries contain small upland lakes.

Even more profound effects on the landscape were caused by ice from the Kenmare Ice Cap, from which large tongues of ice pushed out in all directions. Those moving northwards came up against the barrier of the Macgillycuddys Reeks. The ice split, some pushing westward through Ballaghbeama Pass and down the valley of the Caragh River around to Caragh Lake and Dingle Bay. Cromane Point on Dingle Bay is part of the terminal moraine of this ice flow. Another tongue moved eastwards through

Deep corries such as the Devil's Punch Bowl and the Horse's Glen (shown here) were carved out of the sides of Mangerton and the Reeks by the ice. Many of the corries which were the birth places of the mountain glaciers now contain deep mountain lakes. (Seán Ryan)

Sandstone smoothed and scraped by the glacier which carved out the Killarney valley. (Seán Ryan)

the area south east of Mangerton Mountain. The thickness and pressure of ice was so great that eventually it forced passages through the mountains forming what are known as glacial breaches. Moll's Gap is one such breach, but certainly the most spectacular is the Gap of Dunloe. It was the ice lobe which forced a passage through Moll's Gap which had the greatest impact on the landscape of Killarney National Park. This ice lobe streamed through the low ground of the Owenreagh and Gearhameen river valleys, but as the ice grew thicker it also flowed over much of the surrounding higher ground. The effects of this ice stream are most evident from Ladies View. From here it is easy to see the way in which glacier ice flowing in a trough streamlines and smooths the land surface and widens and deepens its valley. Here the ice has eroded Old Red Sandstone to form a deep wide valley containing glacially scoured lakes (including the Upper Lake) and rock outcrops smoothed into typical shapes known as roches moutonnées.

Once the flow of ice from the Kenmare Ice Cap had pushed north of Torc Mountain it was no longer confined by the high ground on either side and it spread north, west and eastwards in a huge lobe across the lowland which now contains Lough Leane, Killarney town and the River Laune. The predominant ice flow was through the area where Lough Leane now lies pushing westwards along the foot of the Reeks, meeting as it did so the glacier that had pushed through the Gap of Dunloe. The ice had been transporting a vast amount of eroded debris, much of it loosened from the local bedrock by freeze-thaw processes prior to glaciation. This debris was deposited around the edges of the lobe in moraines, some of which were formed by the pushing action of ice, others as fans of sand and gravel deposited by meltwater from the snout of the glacier. The many erratics of Old Red Sandstone on the limestone within the park, particularly on the Muckross Peninsula, show the direction of the ice flow, the nature of the transported material and the extent of the ice. Moraines formed by this ice lobe as far north as Castlemaine and as far west as Glenbeigh show the maximum northern extent of the Kenmare Ice Cap. Although covered in snow for much of the year and with their own, smaller, corrie glaciers, the Macgillycuddys Reeks stood above the main areas of ice and were subjected to intense freeze-thaw activity and subsequent erosion. Much material from their frost shattered slopes found its way down to the glacier's surface to be carried away and deposited elsewhere.

Water expands by 9 per cent when it freezes, with a force sufficient to break open solid rock along lines of weakness. (Padraig O Donoghue)

   The ice cap and its lobes took hundreds and possibly thousands of years to reach this huge size, creeping forward with irresistible force. Then, around 16,000 years ago, the climate became less severe and the ice cap began to melt. The edge of the lobes retreated slowly and unevenly, often stopping or even re-advancing. Even as the extent of the ice lobes shrank, rock debris was still being carried forwards, leaving behind different types of moraines to mark the ice retreat.

   Between 16,000 and 13,000 years ago the climate again deteriorated but was not cold enough to support glaciers. From 13,000 to 10,900 years ago the climate moderated. Large animals including the giant Irish deer

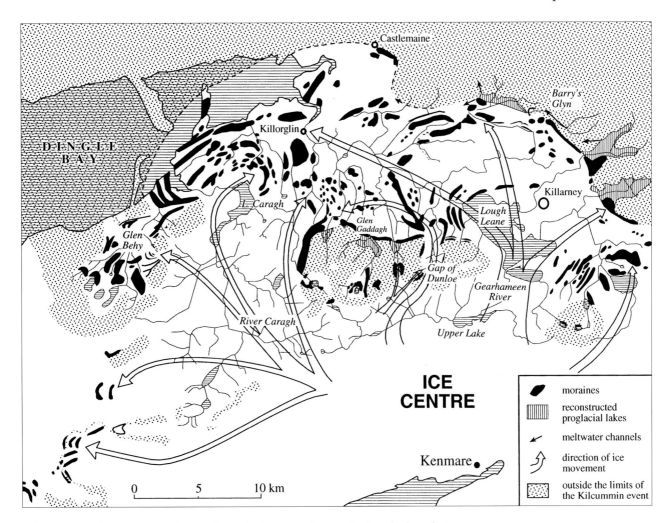

*The extent and movement of ice out from the Kenmare ice cap during the last glacia-
tion (the Midlandian glaciation) is shown by the distribution of moraines within the
area. Although the last glaciation lasted from 120,000 years ago to 10,000 years ago,
this ice advance (known as the LGM or Last Glacial Maximum) probably occurred
between 24,000 and 15,000 years ago and it represents the depths of cold and ice
accumulation during the Midlandian. It was this ice that was responsible for many of
the ice sculpted features that are seen in the Killarney area.*

roamed the area grazing on the rich grassland and herbaceous vegetation. The last glaciation had not quite released its grip, however. Cold polar water in the Atlantic swept past Ireland's coast once more between 10,900 and 10,200 years ago and small glaciers, perhaps up to 300 metres long, grew again in upland corries. These left small end moraines in the corries of the Macgillycuddys Reeks. This deterioration in climate led to the extinction of the giant Irish deer in Ireland.

After the Ice (10,200 years ago to the present day)

From 10,200 years ago the climate became warmer and the Killarney area was transformed by changes in the vegetation described in Chapter 3. Although the colossal forces that were unleashed by the ice ages had gone, the sculpting of the landscape did not cease. Weathering and erosion were slower, but the process of limestone solution continued. Rainwater, water in the soil, and the lake waters are all slightly acidic and this dissolved the limestone. Low cliffs and caves along the limestone shores of the Lower and Middle Lakes have been formed since the last glaciation as have the limestone islands, some undercut to the point where they are supported on legs of limestone. The complex pattern of fissures and crevices formed on the surface of the limestone where it is exposed, particularly on the Muckross Peninsula, are also the result of water dissolving the limestone since the end of the ice age. Deforestation by man left the thin, nutrient-poor soils derived from the sandstone exposed to erosion. In some places only bare rocky hill slopes were left. On level places and gentle slopes where drainage was poor, soils became waterlogged and peat accumulated. Eventually the characteristic cover of blanket bog formed across the landscape.

And so the story of the landscape is never fully told. The imperceptible but unrelenting processes of erosion and weathering continue, the drifting of the tectonic plates goes on, though unnoticeable on the brief scale of human history, and what the future holds for the Killarney landscape we can only guess.

Chapter 3

Woodland History

Richard Bradshaw and Bill Quirke

Killarney's woodlands are wonderfully complex places. The mountains and valleys are ribbed and rutted with smaller ridges, cliffs and gullies, which in turn contain a tangle of boulders from fist size to house size. From under, over and among all this, grows the woodland. But long before you can come to terms with the present reality of the woods your attention will be drawn to the time dimension of these wooded places. Here is a branch ripped from a nearby tree, its leaves not yet withered. Over there is a complete tree blown over, its tangled disc of roots standing three metres tall and still gripping

What were these wooded places like hundreds or thousands of years ago? (Bill Quirke)

A fallen oak regrown.
(Bill Quirke)

chunks of rock; on top of the roots a young birch tree is growing and from the fallen trunk a row of stout new branches reach tall towards the sky. Nearby the shell of a fallen trunk crumbles in your hand. In the woods the past and the dimension of time is almost as immediate as the present. Slowly healing fire scars, multi-trunked pollarded or coppiced trees, regrowth and decay, all speak of the past and draw the mind further and further back. Have the Killarney woodlands always looked the way they do today? What were these wooded places like hundreds or thousands of years ago? These are the questions that a group of research workers from Trinity College Dublin set about answering.

We use information from many sources to discover the plants and animals of former times. Old maps, diaries and paintings have helped in the reconstruction of Killarney, but to explore the time before written records, one has to dig into muddy holes, peat bogs and caves in the hunt for fossil pollen grains, seeds and bones. Pollen grains are produced by all flowering plants, and even though pollen dies within hours of release, its wall can survive for millions of years in a wet, acid place. The surface of each pollen grain has a unique pattern which can be examined under the microscope to reveal the type of plant from which the pollen was released. The deeper one digs, the older are the pollen, seeds and bones that can be found in undisturbed sites, and in this way one can investigate the changing history of the landscape.

All living things contain a minute amount of radioactive carbon. The radioactivity gradually decreases after death, and one can estimate the time since death by measuring the remaining activity. This technique of radiocarbon dating means that a piece of mud can not only reveal what plants grew in the area, but also when they grew. What do these techniques tell us about the history of Killarney National Park?

The Killarney woodlands have not always looked the way they do today. During the 10,000 years that have passed since the end of the last ice age, many different kinds of plants and animals have flourished and then disappeared. Some of the Killarney woodlands have existed for thousands of years and may be called 'ancient woodlands', but the types of trees that composed these woodlands have been changing through time, usually at a rate too slow to be noticeable within a human lifespan.

By 10,000 years ago the warming trend had stabilised, and birch, willow and hazel which survived the last ice age in refuge areas in or close to Ireland were able to respond very rapidly to the dramatic climatic changes that marked the end of glaciation. Birch, willow and hazel formed the first woodlands after the ice retreated. Hazel is rather uncommon in the park today, preferring more fertile soils than those found in the sandstone areas, and more open conditions than occur in the limestone woodlands. The retreating ice left a rich matrix for soil formation, and the first woodlands were open in structure, so hazel flourished. Birch, willow and hazel do not grow tall, live long or cast dense shade so it was only a question of time before taller, longer-lived trees from more distant glacial refuges invaded and formed closed

Woods on the
Muckross Peninsula.
(Paudie O'Leary)

A hazel leaf rimed with
frost. Hazel was an import-
ant tree in the first
Killarney forests after the ice
age. (Padraig O Donoghue)

34

forests. Oak, pine and elm entered the Killarney Valley about 9,000 years ago. The Killarney area was almost completely covered in trees for nearly 3,000 years, even high up in the mountains, where slopes were not too steep. The approaches to the Macgillycuddys Reeks today are over treeless heathlands and peatlands, but 50 cm below the peat surface, abundant birch, willow and hazel pollen show that extensive woodland once blanketed the landscape.

The story of how the present Killarney vegetation came into being differs from place to place. The woods in the remote western side of the park are among the most pristine of upland woodlands to survive in these islands. Large numbers of sensitive mosses and liverworts that can only survive under continuous tree cover grow here. Here we find areas where hazel, ash, yew, willow, mountain ash and alder mix with the oak, unlike many of the more

An ancient alder at Glaisín na Marbh. (Bill Quirke)

accessible woods where oak forms a virtual monoculture. From these remote woods a core of the humus was taken containing nearly 10,000 years of history in the form of pollen grains waiting to be decoded under the microscope. Back in the laboratories, as the pollen was painstakingly extracted from the humus, identified and counted, a fascinating story unfolded. The research results showed that here we have one of Ireland's least ravaged woodlands, and one of the few places that have been continuously forested since the last ice age. An enormous alder tree (6m circumference) stands close to where the humus core was taken, and the pollen in the core showed that alder trees have grown here for over 9,000 years, certainly the oldest alder grove in the country. The first woodlands here after the ice age were of birch, willow and hazel, as elsewhere in the park, but alder and ash also grew, possibly in a sheltered nook by a small stream that flows close by. Grassy glades were frequent and we can imagine red deer grazing these glades and scattering when a family of brown bear or young wolves came to play in the spring sunshine. We can imagine that wild boar liked to root and roll on the muddy banks of the stream where it emerged from the sheltered alder gorge. Spring and summer were hot and dry and lightning strikes led to frequent small forest fires. As you stand today, sheltering from the driving Killarney rain, it is hard to imagine the whole forest burning. Heathland fires started accidentally or deliberately by man are all too common in the park today, but these fires rarely go far into the woodlands. Forest fires were far more frequent between 9,000 and 7,000 years ago, and they left their mark as layers of charcoal deep in the Killarney peat and humus.

Of our native trees scots pine is best adapted to survive fire with its thick resinous bark, and it came into its own when fires were common. Scots pine is the symbol of the forgotten Killarney forests. Pine trees were common in every part of the Killarney valley for several thousand years. Pollen analysis showed that in these upland woods, pine overtopped birch, hazel, and the relatively rare oak, and took over the dominant role from alder for nearly 3,000 years until about 5,000 years ago. These pine forests were probably home to woodpeckers and the turkey-like capercaillie, both no longer found in Ireland. After their 3,000 years of dominance the pine forests finally fell victim to the continuous climatic change that ultimately dictates what grows and moves in Killarney. Cooler, wetter, more familiar summer weather set in

5,000 years ago, and pine seeds did not germinate in the wet, fast growing peat. Many pine trees were engulfed by peat, and their preserved stumps can still be found under the peat as a reminder of the warm pine period.

It was in the Bronze Age that humans began to write themselves into the pollen record of the Killarney valley. The woods became more fragmented and more open than before, and the present pattern of woodland distribution began to develop. The extent of impact varied greatly depending on the accessibility and suitability of the woodland for agricultural activity. Higher woods and woods on steep boulder-strewn slopes would have been safe from the attention of the Bronze Age farmers and their cattle. This was shown in the findings from the western uplands of the park. Here, after the disappearance of the pine, a mixed woodland of alder, birch, hazel and oak, with some yew and ash, continued with little disturbance. However, in the more accessible woods, the picture that emerges is quite different. Research in Camillan wood on the Muckross Peninsula and Derrycunihy wood to the south of the Upper Lake showed scots pine was common in both woods until it disappeared 3,700 years ago from Camillan and 2,300 years ago from Derrycunihy. Human interference through burning and the introduction of grazing animals is apparent in Derrycunihy from this time onwards, and 2,000 years ago it was a rather open heathy place. Since then, the tree flora slowly moved towards the virtual monoculture of oak that we find today. Oak and holly have benefited from years of human disturbance, while pine, ash, alder and willow have been gradually lost. There is more oak in Derrycunihy today than at any other period during the past 5,000 years.

For the last 400 years the history of the woods preserved in the pollen can be interwoven with written records, maps, paintings and engravings. Despite the considerable human impact on the woods of the park in earlier times, when we reach the period of written references to the area we see the Killarney valley and adjacent regions with woods of equal or greater extent than the woods today. This was the time when the old Anglo-Norman and Gaelic power was yielding to direct English rule. One of the earliest written accounts dates from 1584 and describes the confiscated lands of the O'Donoghue Mor of Killarney:

> There are divers timberwoods upon these landes, but no means to make
> commoditie of them by reason that they lie in such remote mountains

An aquatint of the disused smelter at Derrycunihy, engraved by Jonathan Fisher in 1789.

> . . . a great part of these woods consists of oak trees great and small, there are other woods and underwoods in the island of Lough Leane and elsewhere in islands, where grow certain trees called crankanny . . . and there also grow there many yew trees, good for making bows.

Crankanny is an anglicisation of *crann caithne* meaning arbutus tree in the Irish language. The Desmond survey indicates that oak was already predominating in the Killarney woods as is also indicated by the pollen record. The first surviving map of the region is the Down Survey of *c.*1654 made following the Cromwellian re-conquest. Woodland was very restricted in extent, with only Glena Wood marked on the shores of Lough Leane. However, the map does not show unforfeited lands to the east of the Long Range or the area of Tomies Wood and the absence of woods to the south of the Upper Lake is not surprising as the lake itself is only vaguely indicated on the map. The area of Camillan on the Muckross Peninsula is shown as 'coarse pasture' and the pollen record shows a period of abundant heather and low levels of tree pollen several hundred years ago in this area.

Moving into the 1700s there are references to ironworks at Muckross and Derrycunihy. Much timber must have been used to make charcoal for

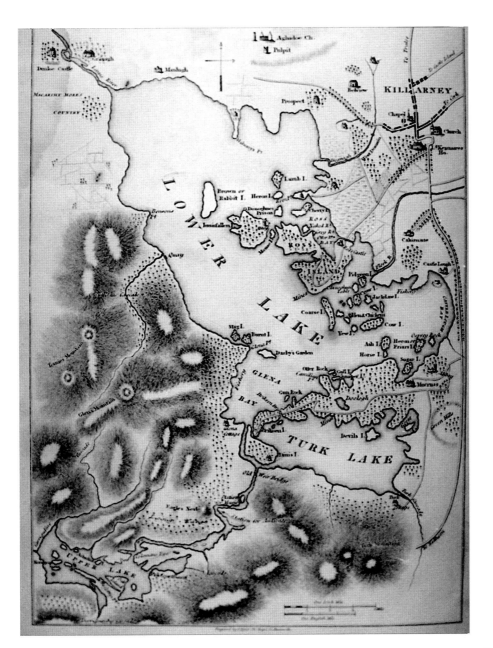

Map of the Killarney Valley 1807. Apart from Tomies Wood on the western side of the Lower Lake, a large proportion of which was felled at that time, the outline of the woods is very similar today. (Isaac Weld, 1807)

39

these works. A further source of forest destruction was the use of oak bark by the tanneries that operated in Killarney in the eighteenth century. Trees will often coppice up again after felling but only if the grazing pressure is not too high. Probably of greater long-term influence than the iron and tanning industries were the pressures exerted by grazing animals. Though less spectacular in their mode of operating, too many grazing animals can destroy a forest more effectively than the axe or the saw. The axe man will not bother to destroy the new shoots that grow up from the fallen stump or the seedling rapidly growing up in the newly cleared area; livestock, on the other hand, will relish them. The Kenmare family papers record that around 1750, three woodrangers were dismissed from service. They had been instructed to keep cattle out of the woods around the Upper Lake, but had:

> not only kept stocks of their own but grazed cattle for others at so much the head and consumed and destroyed my woods at their pleasure.

The iron works appear to have operated for only twenty or thirty years and by the end of the 1700s and the early 1800s when Dunne, Fisher, Young and Weld produced detailed accounts, maps and engravings, the extent of the woodlands in Killarney seems to have been remarkably similar to the extent of woodlands today. The descriptions by Isaac Weld and Arthur Young of the Muckross Peninsula, Tomies Wood and Glena Wood and Jonathan Fisher's engravings of the Upper Lake area would serve quite well to describe these woods today. However, this does not mean that these woods have remained unchanged in the last 200 years because, at the time these authors were writing, some of the woods were suffering very severe exploitation. In 1780 Arthur Young described Derrycunihy wood as:

> part cut down, much of it mangled, and the rest inhabited by coopers, boat-builders, carpenters and turners, a sacrilegious tribe, who have turned the Dryades from their ancient habitations.

In 1807 Isaac Weld gives us a vivid picture:

> When I first visited Killarney, innumerable lights gleamed every evening from the darkened brows of these mountains . . . they proceeded from

Glena Wood today. (Bill Quirke)

Glena Wood 200 years ago. Shortly after the engraving was made the wood was felled but subsequently regrew from coppiced and planted trees. (Engraving by Isaac Weld, 1807)

'A View of the Canal between the Lakes of Killarney from near Colemans Eye the Entrance of the Upper Lake.' *The woods (Cahnicaun) appear the same today. (Print by Jonathan Fisher, 1770)*

The Upper Lake area in 1770. The distribution and appearance of the woodlands remains very similar today. (Print by Jonathan Fisher, 1770)

42

the fires of the people who at that period were engaged in felling the trees and in manufacturing wooden wares, for in this country, instead of bringing the wood to their established work-shops, various artificers, such as coopers, turners, carpenters, hoop makers etc., repair to the forest, in the summer season, and there build themselves huts, in which they reside as long as they find opportunity of providing themselves with materials for exercising their respective trades.

This piecemeal destruction was soon followed by the clear felling of the woods of Glena, Tomies and Ross Island. Limited planting of oak and coppicing of felled trees made good some of the damage. Some planting of new species began. In 1807 a visitor expressed his regret at the sight of a colony of 'Scotchmen' (scots pine) at the base of Torc mountain, but of course they were no strangers to Killarney, and today pine is re-colonising at several locations.

And so we enter the early 1800s with roughly the same extent of woodlands as we see today, some newly replanted, some surviving from earlier times. The replanted woods must have been sufficiently protected from grazing livestock and wild deer to allow them to survive. The trees growing in Tomies Wood, Glena Wood and possibly parts of Looscaunagh Wood (Cahernaduv townland) date from this time. The lack of any trees older than 200 years in these woods is explained by their having been clear felled less than 200 years ago. The lack of very old trees in the other woods is less easy to explain. Were these woods virtually eliminated when the human population increased rapidly between 1800 and 1846? And did they regenerate when the population crashed after the Great Famine? Certainly old cultivation ridges in various parts of the woods indicate that some trees were cleared to make way for cultivation. But these cultivated areas are of limited extent and most of the present woodland area was too rocky and steep to be useful. Paradoxically, scientific examination of tree ages in the park, by counting the annual rings in cores taken from the trees, has shown that in these woods most of the trees date back to the years when the human population was at its highest. In any case there is no evidence in the pollen record or in the written accounts to support the theory that most of the woods were cleared in the early nineteenth century. The account of Mr and Mrs Hall in 1850 indicates that Killarney was abundantly wooded at that time:

Livestock such as cattle and goats appear frequently in eighteenth and early nineteenth century depictions of the Killarney Valley. Large numbers of livestock and deer may have prevented woodland regeneration until the hungry years of the mid-nineteenth century. Top print: goats close to the Upper Lake in 1770; bottom print: cattle along the Long Range River c. 1800. (Top print: Jonathan Fisher 1770, Bottom print Isaac Weld 1807).

The Long Range River circa *1800 (Isaac Weld, 1807)*

The tourist, on approaching the lakes, is at once struck by the singularity and the variety of the foliage in the woods that clothe the hills by which on all sides they are surrounded . . . the road is overhung by huge rocks, each of them is richly clothed – some with huge forest trees, others with the lighter and gayer arbutus.

So we are left with two tantalising questions. If most of these woods have remained intact since the 1700s and earlier, why have none of the individual trees survived from that time? And how did the present generation of trees manage to regenerate at a time when the human population was at its highest and most impoverished? The answers may lie in the insidious impact of grazing by livestock such as cattle, sheep and goats, and wild animals such as deer. For young trees to survive and grow in a woodland, the number of grazing animals must be kept sufficiently low by natural predators such as wolves, by human hunters or by excluding grazing animals from the woodland. It is not known when the last wolf in Killarney was killed, though Charles Smith gives 1710 as the date for the last wolf in Kerry. It seems likely that wolves would not have been sufficiently numerous in Killarney to control grazers after the time of the Tudor conquest of Ireland and the quelling of the

Desmond Rebellion in Kerry in 1583. After this time wolves would have been diligently destroyed, and cattle and goats and perhaps the wild deer would have increased in numbers, preventing the survival of young tree seedlings. If we take this as the last period of truly natural woodland regeneration in Killarney, then by 1800 most of the woods in Killarney would have consisted of trees at least 200 years old. In 1803 Isaac Weld inquired as to why the woods of Ross Island were being felled and was told that:

> the trees had attained their full growth; that many of them had shown symptoms of decay; and that they were declining in value every year.

He received the same account of the woods of Glena. If 200 years ago the Killarney woods were ageing and over mature, it may explain why none of the trees from that time survived to the present time.

This may solve half of our dilemma, but how did the present generation of trees, mostly between 100 and 175 years old, manage to escape the grazers in their vulnerable early years? Somehow conditions favourable to regeneration must have occurred between 1815 and 1890. Were all the woods enclosed? If so it would have been an enormous task, and while the remains of boundary walls can be seen around some of the woods which were replanted, no such remains can be seen around most of the less accessible woods. Were the woods constantly patrolled by gamekeepers and woodrangers to drive the animals out of the woods? Knowing the intricacy of the Killarney woods it seems unlikely that such an effort would be successful either now or in the last century. Could something have happened to the grazers?

A drastic reduction in the number of grazers seems a likely explanation for the woodland regeneration in the nineteenth century. Two factors may have combined to bring this about. The first was a possible reduction in red deer numbers by the owners of the estates; there is at least one account of attempts to control deer in young plantations by driving them towards waiting guns prior to 1842. The second and probably more important factor was the increase in human population. In a 1770 engraving of the Upper Lake by Jonathan Fisher, goats are shown prancing or happily grazing on the steep mountain slopes. In 1780 Arthur Young, writing of Killarney, states that *Great herds of goats are kept on all the mountains*, and as late as 1807 Isaac Weld refers to *immense herds of goats* in the mountains. However, conditions were changing fast, because in the first half of the 1800s the country was undergoing an unprecedented population explosion. Several famines occurred in Ireland before the Great Famine of 1846–1850. In the conditions of dreadful poverty that existed in the early 1800s the people needed three main commodities to survive; their simply constructed cabins, fuel, and food. In the Killarney area turf was plentiful and many old turf banks in the park may date to this time. Fallen wood would also have been plentiful, so the impoverished tenants would probably have avoided felling valuable live trees for fear of eviction. Food was a different matter. When starvation threatened the people, the previously abundant domestic flocks of goats and cattle must have suffered, as must the wild deer population. This left the people depending almost entirely on potatoes, and it probably left the woods relatively free of grazing animals. So, paradoxically, because of the extraordinary increase in human population, the woods, by now decaying and over mature with many open spaces left by fallen trees, may at last have been able to regenerate.

This 'window' of regeneration could have remained open after famine times, because extreme poverty and acute food shortage prevailed, and the woods and mountains of the park became increasingly depopulated after the famine and evictions. It is likely that regeneration finally ended when the red deer increased in number under the strict protection of the game-keepers. The grazing pressure was augmented by Japanese sika deer, which were introduced in 1865 and multiplied prolifically. Later, sheep were introduced to the hills and woods. Any old trees of the 'Tudor' generation, surviving into the late 1800s, would either have died of old age, or their unusual age and size may have attracted the attention of tree fellers, leaving us with the generation of trees that grew up in the 1800s. If this theory is correct, two very distinct generations of trees would have been visible in the middle of the nineteenth century: a generation of trees well over 200 years old, and a generation of very young trees forming an abundant undergrowth which had grown up in the previous few decades. In 1850 Mr and Mrs Hall seem to describe just such a situation along the Long Range river:

Killarney fern. (JJ Earley)

On either side it is amply wooded; patrician trees happily mingled with plebeian underwood, through which glimpses of the huge mountains are occasionally caught.

And along the then newly built road through the Killarney valley:

. . . the lake is hidden, now and then, by intervening trees, and thick masses of underwood . . . Once at least in every furlong you will have to stop . . . noting where the ancient denizens of the woods and forests – the oak, and yew, and holly of centuries old – are mingled with the young growths of yesterday.

These 'young growths of yesterday' have since grown up to form the Killarney forests that we see today, and few if any of the 'ancient denizens' of that time now remain. The future of the Killarney woods will depend on conditions being again created which will allow a new generation to grow up among the ageing trees (see Chapter 12).

Virgin forest is a myth in Killarney. The forests have a long history of human disturbance superimposed on the continuous struggle to cope with climatic change. Killarney woodlands have been impoverished after years of human intervention. The wolf, the boar and the eagle are gone. Our largest filmy fern, still known as the Killarney fern, fell victim to the Victorian passion for ferns and was stripped from every glen and cliff, and hawked about the town in basketfuls. The fern has never recovered, and only survives today in small patches at widely separated localities. Two new introductions, sika deer and rhododendron, threaten the very survival of much of the surviving woodland (see Chapter 12). Rhododendron infestation replaces a rich and diverse biotic community with a poor and monotonous one. The spread of this invasive plant was relatively slow at first. As late as 1939 ecologists could write:

seedlings of Rhododendron are occasionally found far from the parent bushes, but so far invasion of the Killarney woods is mostly marginal.

In 1952 the first clear warning was sounded:

In the Killarney oak woods it is replacing holly as the shrub layer over extensive areas and becoming a menace to the native vegetation (E.F. Warburg).

49

The spread has become a population explosion. By 1969, some 40 per cent of the total area of native woodland had been invaded. In the past two decades, much effort has been put into rhododendron control, and some woods are virtually clear of infestation. Other woods are still choked from end to end by an impenetrable undergrowth, and in other areas the species continues to invade unchecked.

However, the chequered history of woodland disturbance and change has in some ways enriched the park, and human activity has been critical in creating the unusual flora that we preserve in the park today. Arbutus and yew are two of the most fascinating Killarney trees and both may owe their abundance in recent centuries to earlier woodland disturbance. Arbutus is most abundant in the Mediterranean region where fires are common. Its first confirmed appearance in the park is 2,000 years ago, when openings were burned in the forests, and it seems to have been at its most abundant 150–300 years ago when piecemeal interference with the woods was common. Arbutus is now largely confined to the forest margins where it receives sufficient light. The mild winters of Killarney allow arbutus to flourish, which it cannot do in Britain, but it seems to have needed the human intervention in the woods in order to prosper. Yew also flourishes after disturbance, providing grazing is not too severe. Pollen evidence indicates that the impressive Reenadinna Yew wood on the Muckross Peninsula is thousands of years old, dating back to the disturbance resulting from the collapse of the elm tree population after disease, though here again we have the enigmatic absence of very old trees. So a rich mosaic of vegetation types now exists where pure forest once grew. Human activity has unwittingly enriched as well as destroyed. The history of the park is rich and varied, and shows that the present fauna and flora are but one short time frame in the long epic that is Killarney National Park.

Chapter 4

Killarney in Prehistoric Times

William O'Brien

Human settlement of the National Park area may extend back some 10,000 years to the time when the last ice sheets were retreating. It is possible that people lived here even earlier, but if so all traces have been wiped away by the last glaciation. Very little is known of the early inhabitants of this area, as there are virtually no known settlements and few prominent monuments. There has been much destruction of prehistoric sites in the Killarney landscape in recent centuries, while blanket bog and woodland growth restricts the visibility of these remains in the surrounding mountains. Nevertheless, the importance of this area in prehistoric times is clear from the wealth of ancient objects which have been found by local farmers and turf cutters. It is only in recent years that archaeologists have begun to build some picture of this early settlement through systematic survey and excavation.

The First Inhabitants

As the Ice Age came to a close, human groups gradually entered Ireland from about 10,000 years ago, crossing by land bridge connections or open sea from western Britain. With an improving climate, the landscape was gradually transformed from open tundra to dense forest, creating opportunities for the first settlers who survived by hunting wild pig and small game, by fishing in rivers, lakes and along the coast, and by gathering wild plant foods. The earliest evidence of these Mesolithic people in Ireland dates from about 7000 BC and is best known from small encampments investigated in counties Derry and Offaly. In recent years, stone tools made by these first settlers have been discovered in the Blackwater Valley of County Cork and in the Dingle Peninsula of County Kerry. At Ferriter's Cove near Dingle, archaeological excavations have uncovered a coastal settlement dating from between

The invisible people: Mesolithic foragers on the Killarney lake shore 7000–4000 BC? (Drawing: Conor Duggan).

4600–3800 BC, where food was obtained by hunting, fishing from boats and collecting shellfish along the shore.

These early inhabitants had no pottery or metal and depended on stone, wooden and bone tools in their everyday tasks. Flint was particularly valued for the production of axes and blades. However, it is rare in south-west Ireland where other hard rocks such as rhyolite were used. With most Mesolithic sites in Ireland located close to rivers, lakes or the sea, it is likely that the Killarney lakes area was a magnet for settlement at this time. Mesolithic foragers may have settled here on a permanent basis, or visited at certain times to take advantage of seasonally available food resources. In the absence of stone tool finds, the only evidence of Mesolithic settlement in this area comes from a possible hut structure, scientifically dated to around 5500 BC, found during recent archaeological excavations on Ross Island.

The Early Farmers

The period from about 5000–2000 BC saw the slow transition from a mobile hunter-gatherer existence to a way of life where agricultural practices became increasingly important. Farming was gradually introduced into Ireland after 4000 BC, when domesticated cattle and sheep, wheat and barley were brought in probably from Britain or the Continent. The manner of their introduction is not clear, and may have involved the arrival of some migrant populations from abroad. The adoption of agriculture was of major importance in terms of food production and provided the basis for sustained population growth in the Neolithic period between approximately 4000–2000 BC. This growth, together with the demands of an agricultural economy, led to an increasingly settled lifestyle and the emergence of village-type communities such as that identified on the shores of Lough Gur, County Limerick. Specialised craftsmen may have lived in these settlements as this period sees the first appearance of pottery, as well as long distance exchange of stone axeheads and other materials. The use of new types of flint arrowhead reminds us that the hunting of deer and other animals continued to make an important contribution to food supply, as did foraging of coastal, river and lake resources.

The earliest contact with agriculture in County Kerry comes from the late Mesolithic site at Ferriter's Cove in the Dingle Peninsula where cattle bone dating to between 4500–4200 BC has been identified. Indications of early cereal cultivation from the same period have been found in a pollen record taken from a peat bog at Cashelkeelty in south Kerry. While there was some interference with local woodland after 4000 BC, there is no definite evidence of early Neolithic farming in the Killarney area. Agriculture was certainly feasible as much of the lowland area to the east and north of the lakes has fertile soils suitable for cultivation, while even hilly terrain could be used for stock grazing. One explanation for the slow introduction of farming may be that hunting, fishing and gathering plant foods may have represented a very attractive subsistence option in this lakeland environment.

Nonetheless, farming was gradually introduced as pollen records from local bogs indicate an increasing clearance of tree cover in this region after 3000 BC. Initial clearance of woodland would have provided plots for cultivation and paddocks for grazing. Wooden fences or stockades would have been needed to protect the breeding stock from wolf, bear, foxes and human raiders. Several polished stone axeheads found around Killarney probably date to this Neolithic period. As well as small tillage patches cleared close to the houses, much effort would have gone into breaking the forest canopy with these axes to form rough grazing for the growing herds of cattle. In this way, early farmers slowly transformed the landscape around Killarney to create an organised farmscape of field systems and settlements in areas of suitable soil cover. While these were mostly cleared away by subsequent farming, many hill bogs in the Kerry peninsulas preserve field walls and enclosures from this period covering large areas of land.

Population growth through secure food supply and increasingly fixed patterns of settlement saw tribal territories appear across the Cork-Kerry region by 2500 BC. This link with the land was further expressed through religious beliefs which centred on ancestor worship and fertility rituals performed at megalithic tombs. In many areas, small farming communities developed a strong local identity based on the use of large stone monuments. While no examples are known from the Killarney area, numerous megalithic tombs have been found in Cork and Kerry. These include a small number of passage tombs, distant cousins of the more spectacular monuments built around 3100 BC in the Boyne Valley of County Meath, including a possible example recently excavated at Ballycarty near Tralee. More numerous are the many small wedge-shaped tombs found in the south-western peninsulas, the distribution of which reflects a widespread adoption of farming and a growing population in this region after 2500 BC. While the Cork-Kerry tombs lack the ornate decoration of passage tombs like Newgrange, there are numerous examples of cup-and-ring art in the Iveragh and Dingle Peninsulas. An example of this art, now destroyed, was located at Gortboy to the north of Carrauntohill. Many of the hill-top cairns found in the mountains around Killarney and further east to the Paps may have been the burial sites of important people from this later Neolithic period.

The Years of Bronze and Gold

After perhaps 2,000 years of farming with stone, wood, bone and antler tools, the art of mining and working metal was brought to Killarney. The earliest metal objects include gold ornaments in the form of discs and collars, as well as copper axes, daggers and halberds. At first, metal objects were scarce which, together with their obvious aesthetic value, made them the prestigious possessions of the most powerful in society. Two gold collars or lunulae from the Killarney area are outstanding examples of metalworking expertise at this time. One of these was found on Mangerton mountain, while the other was discovered in the eighteenth century in the Kenmare

55

estate, close to the modern town. These crescentic collars of gold sheetwork were an early Irish initiative and represent a high point of European gold working in this period. The lunulae, with their incised patterns of triangles, lozenges and chevrons, are powerful symbols of authority and prestige. The two Killarney examples are likely to indicate the existence of a powerful leadership in this area around 2000 BC.

The art-style represented on these lunulae is generally linked to the decoration found on a type of pottery called Beaker ware which appeared in Ireland around 2400 BC. This Beaker pottery is found in most regions of western Europe where it generally marks the end of the Neolithic and the first widespread adoption of metallurgy. While many scholars interpret the spread of Beaker pottery and an associated range of quality artifacts, including metalwork, as the trading of prestige items between different regions, others continue to believe in the migrations of ethnic groups from the continent who introduced the knowledge of metallurgy to Britain and Ireland. It does seem that the appearance of this pottery in Ireland around 2400 BC coincided with the introduction of copper and gold objects.

Five copper axeheads have been found in the Killarney area dating to this early metal-using period. These include a hoard of three axeheads found by a farmer ploughing at Cullinagh above Tomies Wood in 1868 and an example from Muckross. The early use of unalloyed copper was followed by the development of tin-bronze metallurgy in Ireland by 2100 BC. Several early bronze axes have been found in the Killarney area, including one example from Knockasarnet which was discovered together with an ingot of raw copper in a bog. Recent research confirms that these and other copper-bronze objects were being made in the Killarney area between 2400–1800 BC, using copper ore deposits mined at Ross Island. This mine appears to have been a major source of early copper and was among the first places where metal was actually produced in Ireland.

Ross Island

This early copper mine on Lough Leane has a long history of mining, beginning around 2400 BC in the final stages of the Neolithic and continuing into later times. The Welsh monk Nennius, writing around 800 AD, probably had this location in mind when he listed the mineral wealth of this area as one of the wonders of the known world:

> There is a lake called Loch Lein. Four circles are around it. In the first circle, it is surrounded by tin, in the second by lead, in the third by iron, in the fourth by copper, and in the lake many pearls are found that kings place in their ears.

The mine workings at Ross Island occur in a copper-rich stratum of the Lower Carboniferous limestone. This mineralisation was the focus of mining in several periods, beginning with Early Bronze-Age operations between 2400–1800 BC. Mining continued in the early medieval period, possibly contemporary with the writings of Nennius, and can be recognised in the discovery of several smelting furnaces at Ross Island. The Browne family, owners of the Kenmare estate, encouraged prospecting here in the eighteenth century, which eventually led to an important mining operation between 1804–1829, during which time some 4,000 tons of copper ore were shipped to the Swansea smelters.

These eighteenth- and ninteenth-century miners at Ross Island uncovered older primitive workings, described then as 'Danes Mines' following the antiquarian tradition of that era. These mines and the numerous stone hammers from the site were the object of much curiosity in the Victorian era. Early tourist and visitor accounts record 'chambers of rudely vaulted form', worked by '. . . kindling large fires on the limestone, thereby reducing it to a caustic state'. It was generally assumed that these ancient workings were destroyed in the nineteenth-century mining. However, recent investigations by a research team from National University of Ireland, Galway have identified surviving traces.

The Bronze Age workings at Ross Island appear as large cave-like openings on mineralised exposures in the limestone. The mine walls have a smooth concave profile indicative of fire-setting, where wood-fuelled fires were lit against the rock face to fracture the mineralised limestone. Stone cobble hammers were then used, both hafted and hand-held, to pound the fire-weakened face and remove rock. These miners tunnelled underground from these cave openings, to depths not exceeding ten metres across the site. They did experience problems with flooding as much of the ore-bearing

Beaker/Early Bronze Age copper mine at Ross Island, 2400–1800 BC. *(William O'Brien)*

ground here is under lake level. This was also a problem in the ninteenth century when steam engines were used to pump water from mine shafts inside a large coffer dam built around the site.

A large deposit of broken rock spoil has been identified around the Bronze Age mine workings. This spoil is rich in charcoal from the mine fires and contains a large number of stone hammers, carefully grooved to take withy handles. Other items of mine equipment include the shoulder-blade bones of cattle used as scoops or shovels to move crushed rock around the site in baskets of some type. This broken rock was initially sorted close to the mine workings to separate barren limestone from the mineralised fragments which were then taken for concentration.

Copper smelting pits at Ross Island, 2400–1800 BC. (William O'Brien)

Of particular importance is the discovery of a work camp adjacent to these early mine workings which can be dated to between 2400–1800 BC. This site contains an ore-processing area where metal was made and the remains of wooden huts where miners sheltered, cooked food and engaged in other activities. Food waste in the form of animal bone fragments, and pebble flint working, and evidence of hunting in the form of a flint arrowhead attest to other activities in the life of this mining camp. The animal bones, mostly cattle with some pig and sheep, point to an important agricultural base supporting the mine operation, probably located within the environs of Killarney. These bones, dating to between 2400–1800 BC, represent the earliest evidence of farming which we presently have for this area.

59

It is not certain whether the mining at Ross Island was organised on a seasonal basis or involved a long-term commitment by full-time miners. Excavation of the Bronze Age work camp uncovered spreads of mine limestone finely crushed using stone hammers and anvil slabs. Careful hand-sorting was required to concentrate this copper ore, possibly using some form of water flotation to separate finer fractions. The ore concentrate was then reduced to metal, by smelting at high temperatures in pit furnaces to produce metal droplets. These were subsequently re-melted to form ingots which were then taken from the site, probably to permanent settlements in the Killarney area and beyond, where this metal was used in the fabrication of artifacts. The pit furnaces from Ross Island are the first Bronze Age copper smelters to be identified in Ireland. The metal produced here had a distinctive arsenical composition derived from the natural chemistry of the Ross Island copper ores. This arsenic content is useful in tracing the circulation of Killarney metal to other regions, through trade and other exchanges. It appears that axeheads, daggers and other objects made from this copper were exchanged widely across Ireland, with some examples even reaching western Britain.

Radiocarbon dates place the earliest activity at Ross Island in the period 2400–2200 BC, making this the oldest copper mine presently known in north-western Europe. Particularly significant is the discovery of Beaker pottery in this mine camp site. These small pottery vessels, decorated with simple cord and comb impressions, were used as drinking cups by the miners. Ross Island is the first copper mine in Europe that can be directly linked to the metalworking activity of these 'Beaker Folk' and thus to the origins of Irish metallurgy.

A Bronze Age Landscape

Encouraged by the mineral wealth of Ross Island and the many subsistence opportunities offered by the mountains, lakes and agricultural lowlands, there was extensive human settlement in the Killarney area between 2400–600 BC. This Bronze Age period saw the widespread disappearance of the dense woodlands which covered much of Ireland in earlier times. Pollen records indicate that there was an increasing area of land under cultivation and pasture, facilitated possibly by the introduction of ploughing. Though no sites have been excavated in Killarney, it is likely that these Bronze Age people still lived in simple settlements, consisting of small groups of huts surrounded by fenced or ditched enclosures to protect themselves and their livestock. Closely related to such settlements are the many *fulachta fiadh* or burnt mound sites known from this period. These are generally visible as a low mound or spread of fire-shattered stone and charcoal, often exposed during ploughing. Excavation generally reveals a wood-lined trough, in which water was boiled by immersing hot stones from a nearby hearth. Meat and other foods were cooked in this pit for consumption at nearby habitations. At least twenty of these burnt mounds have been identified to the immediate north of Killarney town, extending east from Fossa, along the Aghadoe Heights, to the Tullig-Dooneen area.

The period after 1500 BC saw a general expansion of settlement across the Cork-Kerry region, marked archaeologically by a proliferation of new ritual monuments including stone circles and rows, single standing stones, boulder burials and cairns. These free-standing megaliths combined rites of cremation burial with new rituals centred on the worship of heavenly bodies. There are numerous examples of such sites in the Iveragh and Dingle Peninsulas of County Kerry. However, they are less frequent around Killarney. The most important site here is the stone circle at Lissyviggeen, to the east of Killarney

Ingot of Ross Island copper and bronze axehead from Killarney area, 2100–2000 BC. (National Museum of Ireland)

61

town. This site consists of a small circle of seven stones, surrounded by an earthen bank with a pair of outlying stones. Though not dated, this monument is believed to lie within the henge tradition of monuments in Ireland and Britain, the most famous example being Stonehenge itself. Other Bronze Age ritual monuments include many of the single standing stones found around Killarney, including the large roadside example at Fossa.

The period between 1200–600 BC witnessed an enormous growth in metal production in Ireland, completing the transition from a stone-dependent economy to one in which metal was widely used for everyday tasks. The Late Bronze Age is marked by an abundance of gold objects of great complexity and beauty, such as three penannular bracelets and gold dress fasteners found in a wooden box at Kilmoyly bog near Ballybunion, County Kerry. A darker side to this wealth is reflected in the increasing production of bronze weaponry such as spearheads, swords and shields. An important discovery in the Killarney area is the large hoard of bronze trumpets found in a local bog in 1835–6. These sophisticated objects are often viewed as war trumpets, while others see their use in a largely ritual context, which may have involved their deliberate destruction as votive offerings in lakes and bogs.

Celts and Ironworkers

The spread of Celtic culture and language after 300 BC took place at a time of considerable political instability in Ireland, marked by inter-tribal conflicts. Some believe that this was due to pressures on food supply, which

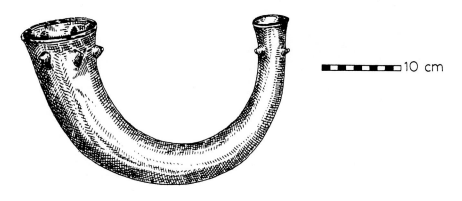

Late Bronze Age trumpet found with several others in a Killarney bog, dating from 800–500 BC.

began early in the first millennium BC when climate began to deteriorate leading to problems with soil fertility and bog development. The centuries after 600 BC saw the first contacts with the iron-using world of the continental Celts. This is marked in County Kerry by the discovery of a Late Bronze Age hoard containing a bronze bracelet of French Hallstatt origin from Kilmurry near Castleisland. Also significant is the discovery of a wooden replica of a Celtic sword from a bog at Cappagh in the Iveragh Peninsula. The concentration of wealth under force of arms is seen in the increasing tendency to build defended settlement enclosures on hill-tops and lakesides. The construction of these hillforts reflects the centralisation of power and possibly the emergence of tribal federations. The militarism of these societies is echoed in early heroic sagas such as the *Táin*, where warrior castes are continuously engaged in inter-tribal warfare and territorial disputes.

Little is known about the Killarney area in this Iron Age period. No Iron Age strongholds comparable to the inland promontory fort of Caherconree in the Dingle peninsula or the large enclosure at Glanbane near Tralee have been found. A recent excavation at Lissyviggeen stone circle did reveal evidence of fires dating to the first century AD, possibly associated with later

Bronze Age stone circle, Lissyviggeen, Killarney. (William O'Brien)

63

Ogham stone found in a souterrain in the Dunloe area, near Beaufort, Killarney. (William O'Brien)

Celtic rituals at this Bronze Age site. The centuries which followed saw the appearance of numerous ringforts, small settlement enclosures of earth or stone, in the Killarney area. Construction of these single-family farmsteads commenced in the pagan Iron Age and increased with the social fragmentation of the centuries leading up to and following the introduction of Christianity. Most of the ringforts found in the Killarney area have single earthen bank and ditch defences, which would have been strengthened by timber palisades, enclosing a complex of timber-built houses and domestic areas. There are many examples of souterrains or underground tunnel systems in these ringforts, including two examples in the Muckross area of the National Park.

Contacts with the Roman world may have been responsible for the introduction of the Ogham script into Kerry in the early centuries AD. The most important Ogham discovery in the Killarney area was made in 1838 when seven inscribed stones were found in a souterrain at Coolmagort near the Gap of Dunloe. Ogham is the earliest form of Old Irish known and is essentially a cipher based on the Latin alphabet. It was generally used for commemorative inscriptions on stone pillars, such as those found in the famous 'cave of Dunloe' where one inscription can be translated to read 'the stone of the son of Ttal the son of Vorgos the son of the kindred of Toicaci'. While Ogham may represent the earliest vestige of literacy in these pagan Iron Age societies, the prehistoric period is finally brought to an end by the introduction of Christianity to the Killarney area, possibly as early as the fifth century AD. With the first Christian missionaries came books and writing and eventually recorded history.

Chapter 5

FROM THE EARLY CHURCH TO THE FOUNDATION OF THE NATIONAL PARK

Grellan D. Rourke

The Early Church

Inisfallen is the largest island on Loch Leane. Today the island seems suspended between the wild wooded mountains to the west and the inhabited lowlands to the east. It is here at the edge of the wild lands, haunt of wolves, eagles and deer, that St Fionán Lobhar (the Leper) is reputed to have founded his monastery in the late sixth or early seventh century. For the early monks the island provided some protection, fertile soil and most importantly peace and seclusion for contemplation and prayer. The founding of Inisfallen monastery, and its sister monastery overlooking the lake from the hill of Aghadoe to the north, ushered in the age of Christianity and written history. It also marked the beginning of almost 1,000 years of monastic occupation of the island.

During the fifth century St Patrick and his missionaries established an episcopal church based on dioceses, but by the early sixth century the monastic movement had engulfed this organisation. This may have been because the monastic movement fitted more easily with the Gaelic civil structure, which was decentralised and rural. Throughout Ireland, monasteries were founded by holy men such as St Fionán. Inisfallen and the other early monasteries would have consisted of one or more small churches, small cells where the monks lived, and other structures for animals and stores. The earliest buildings were made of timber and the monasteries were structured to suit each individual community and location, with no definitive pattern to their layout. Land was cleared to grow vegetables such

Inisfallen where St Fionán Lobhar (the Leper) is reputed to have founded his monastery in the late sixth or early seventh century. (Bill Quirke)

Romanesque doorway on Inisfallen. (Dúchas)

as kale, carrots, leeks and onions, and fish from the lake would have featured in the monks diet.

With the passage of time the monastery grew in importance. A monastic school was established and the monastery became an important centre of influence in the region. Monasteries often provided vital services to the outside community. In the late ninth century, the monks of Inisfallen built a hospital or *noscomium*, probably for lepers. The monastery would have acquired the right of sanctuary for both people and property, and rapidly accumulated land and wealth. Masterpieces such as the Ardagh Chalice and the Book of Kells show the wealth and craftsmanship of the Irish monasteries at this time. This growth in prosperity eventually attracted the attention of marauding Vikings who appeared in Kerry at the end of the eighth century. No written account of Viking raids on the Killarney monasteries has come down to us, but it seems unlikely that these monasteries would have escaped the fate of so many other monasteries throughout the country. Once the bows of Viking boats beached on the rocky shores of Inisfallen, the monastery would have been defenceless. Sacred relics would have been desecrated, valuables stolen, buildings burnt and the monks killed or kidnapped.

Such attacks on monasteries span a period of several hundred years. Raiding was not confined to the Vikings as, later on, Irish tribes frequently plundered the monasteries. Repeated destruction of timber structures may well have persuaded the monks to construct more durable buildings of stone. In the middle of the eleventh century the Annals of Inisfallen refer to such an early stone church or *daimhliag* at the monastery of Aghadoe which overlooked Lough Leane from the northeast. Part of this early church can still be seen at the north-west corner of the present cathedral where the wall is built with distinctively larger stones. Round towers were constructed at this time and the remains of a round tower can still be seen at Aghadoe. These towers were used not only as belfries but as look-out towers and places of refuge in times of attack.

The Medieval Church

By the eleventh century the great days of early monasticism were coming to an end, and at the close of this century church reform had already begun. As

Drawing of Romanesque doorway at Aghadoe (1892).

a consequence the early twelfth century ushered in a period of church building, and the need for diocesan cathedrals stimulated the adoption of the Romanesque style which the Irish adapted to incorporate some of their own very distinctive patterns and motifs.

Magnificent examples of the decorative sandstone carved during this period can be seen at both Aghadoe and Inisfallen. The Aghadoe church, built in 1198 by the O'Donoghues, exhibits very intricate, almost exotic designs, while the doorway on Inisfallen displays fine chevron ornament with zig-zag moulding above. Such work was carried out by very skilled craftsmen and reflected the power and wealth of such communities. It was one of the most exciting, imaginative and expressive periods of Irish architecture.

During this period of reform the monasteries of Aghadoe and Inisfallen developed in different directions. While Aghadoe became part of the new parochial structure with cathedral status, Inisfallen adopted the rule of the Canons Regular of St Augustine and became known as the Priory of St Mary.

This priory subsequently expanded in a more formal way. The church was extended and the usual monastic buildings were constructed around a courtyard called a cloister garth. Soon, in accordance with recent innovation, chancels (the part containing the altar, sanctuary and choir) were added to the churches at both Aghadoe and Inisfallen.

The scale of the buildings is small, but despite its size the priory became a major seat of learning and it was here that the Annals of Inisfallen were compiled. This document is a valuable source for early Irish history and is now in the care of the Bodleian Library, Oxford. The monks of Inisfallen included artists and craftsmen of great skill and the Inisfallen crozier is but one example of the quality of art of this period. The crozier, now in the National Museum in Dublin, is made of wood covered in ornamental silver. It was found in a nearby river in 1867. Monastic wealth was still vulnerable in medieval times. A raid by the O'Donoghues in 1180 is described in the Annals of Inisfallen:

> There was committed in this year a deed which greatly vexed the clergy of all Ireland, namely the plundering of InisFaithleann by Mael Duin, son of Domnall Ua Donnachada, and the carrying off by him of

Detail of Stone carving from Inisfallen. (Dúchas)

all the worldly wealth therein, which was under the protection of its saints, clerics, and consecrated churches. He collected, indeed, the gold, silver trappings, mantles and cloakes of Iar Mumhan, without any respect for God or man, but the mercy of God did not allow him to kill people or to strip this heavenly place of church furnishings or books.

The Norman Conquest and the Gaelic Revival

By the mid thirteenth century, the McCarthys and their subordinate clans, the O'Sullivans and O'Donoghues, had been pushed by the Anglo-Normans into the extreme south and southwest of the country. This push was finally halted by two battles in which the McCarthys defeated the Anglo-Normans; the first in 1260 at Callen near Kenmare and the second in 1261 at Tuairín Cormac on the slopes of Mangerton just east of the national park. The Norman invaders constructed defensive structures both in timber and stone to consolidate their fragile hold on the lands that they held. They constructed castles at Dunloe and Aghadoe. Two storeys are all that remain of the circular Norman keep at Aghadoe, also known as Parkavonear Castle. The stairs and passageways are built within its massive walls and the remains of a fireplace can still be seen on the upper floor. This

Ross Castle in 1796 aquatint by T. Walmsley.

tower stands within an earthen enclosure with projecting bastions to the south and was originally surrounded by a dry moat.

By the late thirteenth century the Anglo-Normans had lost their grip and Dunloe Castle came into the hands of the O'Sullivan Mór clan who retained it as their stronghold for almost 400 years. What became of the keep at Aghadoe is not certain, but it may have become the bishop's residence.

The fourteenth century witnessed the revival of the old feudal ways and of Gaelic literature and learning. During this period the local clans consolidated their power in Kerry and the central power of the Church increased. It was also a period of economic depression with several outbreaks of famine and the Black Death. Consequently there was very little building. However, renewed prosperity during the fifteenth century resulted in the building of the Friary of Irrelagh and Ross Castle, both within the park.

The friary of Irrelagh (*Oirbhealach* meaning the eastern passage), also known as Muckross Abbey, was founded for the Observantine Franciscans in 1448 by the McCarthy Mór. Tradition says it was built on the site of an earlier

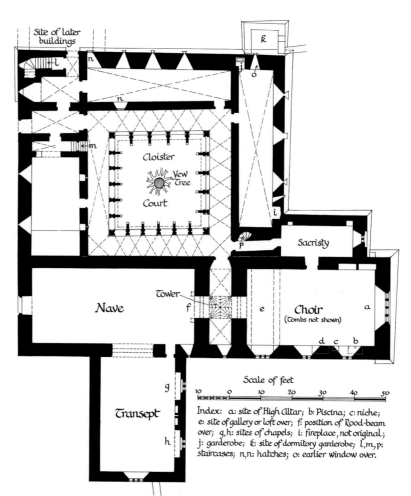

Site of later buildings

Cloister

Yew Tree

Court

Sacristy

Nave

Tower

Choir
(Tombs not shown)

Transept

Scale of feet

10   0   10   20   30   40   50

Index: a: site of High Altar; b: Piscina; c: niche;
e: site of gallery or loft over; f: position of Rood-beam
over; g,h: sites of chapels; i: fireplace, not original;
j: garderobe; k: site of dormitory garderobe; l,m,p:
staircases; n,n: hatches; o: earlier window over.

Plan of the ground floor
Muckross Abbey
by H.G. Leask.

church which had been destroyed by fire. It was a large project which could
only have been executed at a time of great faith and stability. The Gothic
structures took 50 years to finish and the south transept was the last phase of
work to be completed. The nave and chancel are almost completely separated by a later tower which was not part of the original design. The friary was
finished to a high standard although the decorative work is quite restrained;
perhaps this is due to the hardness of the limestone used. An austere cloister
lies to the north. This cloister is buttressed, a feature of many fifteenth-
century Irish monasteries. Around the cloister are vaulted apartments above

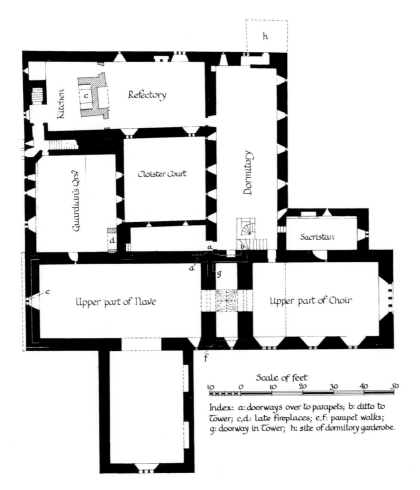

Plan of the upper level of Muckross Abbey by H.G. Leask.

which are the abbot's apartment, refectory, dormitory and other rooms. An ancient yew tree still grows in the cloister. Most of the monastery is remarkably still intact today.

Not everywhere, however, was experiencing renewed religious zeal and, at the time Muckross Abbey was being constructed, the Priory of St Mary on Inisfallen was in decline. Religious rule there had become very lax and in 1461 the prior was said to have been living with a concubine. Only seventeen years later a Donal O'Shea was acting as prior without papal authority and he and his canons were apparently living outside the monastery.

Ross Castle on the shore of Lough Leane was built in the fifteenth century and served as the defensive stronghold of the O'Donoghues for about 100 years. This photograph shows the castle before its recent restoration. (Bill Quirke)

At this time the O'Donoghue clan had undisputed hold over the Killarney area and set about constructing Ross Castle on the shore of Lough Leane. This substantial castle was their defensive stronghold for about 100 years. The keep was defended by a small outer wall fortified with circular flanking towers, two of which are still intact. The castle is austere in design with little decoration. It was altered in the later sixteenth century, perhaps around the time of the Desmond rebellion. This was done to improve the defences; two corner bartizans were added to the battlements and musket opes were inserted. Most of the original battlements had gone but they would have been similar to those at Muckross Abbey and Ballycarbery Castle, near Cahirciveen.

Ross Castle would not have stood in isolation; associated with it would have been many timber structures where the Chieftain's retinue lived. The keep itself has a typical plan with a stone spiral staircase and small chambers located at one end and the main chambers at the other. The principal room, O'Donoghue's dining hall, is located on the top floor and this would have been where the Chieftain had his court and held his banquets. At one end there was a timber gallery where the musicians played. This castle has now been fully restored and houses a fine collection of old oak furniture.

The Consolidation of the English Conquest

With the passage of time the leading Anglo-Normans of south Munster, the Earls of Desmond, had adopted the Irish way of life and intermarried with local families. However, with the establishment of direct English rule in the sixteenth century, the pendulum began to swing back. In 1536 the Dublin Parliament legally dissolved the monasteries and six years later the Earl of Desmond was commissioned to dissolve the religious houses in Kerry, although there seems to have been no real interference with the monasteries here at that time.

Then followed the Desmond rebellion which began in 1569 and continued until 1583 when the Earl of Desmond was finally killed. During these wars Dunloe Castle was assaulted and suffered considerable damage. The O'Donoghue Ross had taken the losing side which cost him his life and the subsequent forfeiture of his lands. A survey was commissioned by the Crown of the fallen rebels' lands and one of the surveyors, Sir Valentine Brown, benefited greatly from the subsequent land confiscations. O'Donoghue's lands and castle passed briefly into the hands of Donal MacCarthy Mór, but being chronically short of money he mortgaged them to Sir Valentine Browne. Due to the collapse of the MacCarthy fortunes soon afterwards the castle came into Browne's hands, although it was the subject of litigation for some time thereafter.

Shortly after the Desmond Rebellion, in 1589, English soldiers in the area ravaged the priory at Inisfallen which had probably been abandoned by this time. They also raided Muckross Abbey and killed two of the friars. A few years later Queen Elizabeth I granted the revenue of both these monasteries to a Captain Robert Collum but subsequently the lands at Inisfallen were granted to Sir Valentine Browne in 1613. The Browne family, later to become Earls of Kenmare, became Catholic and turned a blind eye to continued religious activity, for Inisfallen appears to have been reoccupied by the monks in 1633. At Muckross Abbey also the friars moved back for a brief occupation in 1602. A further occupation took place ten years later when the old buildings were partially restored under the direction of Rev Thaddeus Houlihan. The friars had to abandon their monastery again in 1629 due to religious persecution but they returned one last time before leaving for good when the Parliamentary Army occupied Kerry.

By 1641 revolt had broken out all over Ireland and eventually Cromwell's forces arrived to quell the rebellion. When the Parliamentary Army finally arrived in Kerry in 1652, under the command of General Ludlow, they attacked Dunloe Castle and a great portion of it was demolished during the subsequent bombardment. Castle Lough, the fortress of the MacCarthy Mór on Lough Leane, was also besieged and when it was taken, the structure was substantially demolished. Ross Castle was held by Lord Muskerry when General Ludlow laid siege to it with infantry and horsemen. The castle surrendered when Ludlow brought artillery by boat up the river

Aerial view of Muckross House. (Dúchas)

78

Laune across Lough Leane; it was one of the last major strongholds to yield during the Cromwellian wars. The Parliamentary Army caused much misery and destruction in Ireland. Both Muckross Abbey and Inisfallen Priory were burned and evidence of this destruction is still plainly visible today in the damaged stonework. After 1652 both monasteries were abandoned for good, finally closing an important chapter of Irish history.

The Period of the Ascendancy

Both the Browne and Herbert families, the owners of the two great estates of Killarney up to recent times, had moved to Kerry to take up confiscated land. They were termed 'undertakers' because they undertook to settle the land with English Protestant farmers. The Brownes received extensive confiscated lands in the area after the Desmond Rebellion and Sir Valentine Browne established himself at Ross Castle, building himself a fortified house alongside the castle in 1688. Not long after, at the time of the Williamite Wars, Ross Castle became a permanent military post and was converted to a barracks. The garrison at Ross also made use of Browne's quarters for which he was eventually compensated. A more permanent barracks was built adjoining the castle in the mid eighteenth century and this accommodated two companies of infantry and a governor. When the garrison was finally removed around 1825, Lord Kenmare had the roof of the barracks removed and the large windows altered to loops to reflect the style of the castle.

At the time of the Desmond forfeitures Killarney town was a small settlement. The Earls of Kenmare were responsible for the early development of the town and by the early seventeenth century it had become a plantation market town with 40 houses built and occupied by English planters. In the 1720s the Kenmares built a large but undistinguished house at Kenmare Place in Killarney town. By the 1750s the town began to be developed as a destination for visitors, perhaps the first of its kind in Ireland, and Lord Kenmare implemented many improvements. One dubious 'improvement' was the conversion of the church on Inisfallen in 1760 to a banqueting hall for the reception of visitors to the 'romantic scenes' of Kerry which for about 50 years remained one of the most important tourist attractions.

The cloister of Muckross Abbey. (Dúchas)

The house at Kenmare Place was eventually demolished when Killarney House was built close to the town at Knockreer between 1875 and 1881. This was subsequently destroyed by fire in 1913 and the family returned to Kenmare Place where the last Earl died. He was succeeded by his niece, Beatrice Grosvenor, who built a new house at Knockreer in 1958.

The Herbert family, though they had received lands in Kerry, only leased the Muckross Estate from the MacCarthy Mór. However, it finally came into their possession when Charles MacCarthy Mór, whose mother was a Herbert, died in 1770 bequeathing his estate to his uncle. Like the Brownes, they had a passion for building new houses and three houses were built on the Muckross Estate before the present Muckross House, each in a different location. Their third mansion was taken down in 1837 and the remains of its basement can still be seen on the estate.

The present house was built in 1843 to a design by Mr William Burn, a prominent Scottish architect. The house is neo-Elizabethan in style and very imposing with large mullioned windows. It is faced with Portland stone which was first shipped to Cork and then transported over the mountains to Muckross. At the time it cost £30,000. Financial problems eventually forced the Herberts to sell the estate in 1899. The new owner, Lord Ardilaun, in turn sold it to Mr and Mrs W.B. Bourn who gave it as a wedding present to their daughter Maude and her husband Arthur Vincent. In 1932 Arthur Vincent, together with his parents-in-law, gave the Muckross Estate to the Irish nation as a national park, called the Bourn Vincent Memorial Park, in memory of his late wife.

The other great Killarney estate, the Kenmare Estate, remained in private ownership until 1972, when the Irish Government commenced a series of property acquisitions by gift and purchase from the owners of the estate, Mrs Grosvenor and Mr McShain. These culminated in the purchase of most of the remainder of the Kenmare Estate, following the death of Mrs Grosvenor in 1985 and the acquisition of Derrycunihy Wood from Coillte (the state forestry company) in 1993.

Chapter 6

THE PEOPLE OF THE GLENS

Bill Quirke

The low hill of Knockreer rises just west of Killarney town. From here you can see the national park stretching away to the south. Woodland seems to fill the valley, broken only by glimpses of the lake. The converging mountain flanks of Mangerton and Torc to the southeast, and Tomies, Shehy and Eagle's Nest to the southwest seem to direct the lowlands and the eye towards the cliffy face of Cromaglan 10 km away. Off to your left, outside the park, a few houses can be seen, but the great expanse of mountains, lakes and woods in front of you seems empty, but for the grey ruined block of Ross Castle rising among the distant trees. At night it is completely dark out there. A late car on the mountainy road from Kenmare emphasises the emptiness with a brief bright pinpoint of light.

Is this the last primeval land in Ireland? Many on first acquaintance have been tempted to think so. Miles of native forests and herds of red deer, survivors from ancient times, tell a story unique in Ireland, but Killarney National Park has many stories to tell. One story has never been written down; vague rumours of it have been passed by word of mouth and can be heard from some of the older people who have lived close to the park all their lives. The story can now only be reconstructed from accounts of travellers who visited here between 150 and 250 years ago, from sparse official records and maps, and most of all from the stones and soil of the mountains and woods. It is the story of the last inhabitants of the Killarney mountains.

The old road from Killarney to Kenmare curves westwards to flank the high mountain group of Mangerton, Dromderalough and Knockrower. For 15 miles it makes its way through hills and lower mountain passes to Kenmare town. Deserted now, and in places obliterated by the slowly growing bog, it is along this old road that we will begin to construct our story. On a summer day, with the bracken fern growing high along the road, the

Left. The old road to Kenmare where it passes between Torc and Mangerton mountains. (Bill Quirke)

Right. The old road to Kenmare in Esknamucky Glen. (Bill Quirke)

overwhelming impression is of wildness; wild mossy woods and wild mountains. But if we bide our time and return this way on a sunny evening in late winter or early spring, the soil and rocks will begin to tell their story. With startling clarity the low evening light conjures up a ghostly landscape. The dense growth of bracken fern has died back over the winter and here and there the low sun reveals ridges etched in the ground, like giant ripples in the soil. The eye begins to pick out low, tumbled stone walls. In the woods, grassy terraces stand out from the surrounding forest floor which is scattered with moss-cushioned boulders. As you approach, a confusion of these moss-covered stones may resolve itself into the roofless walls of a tiny one-roomed cabin, blanketed in moss. Above the woods on the exposed mountain-side,

The ruins of a one-roomed house covered with moss in Ullauns Wood. (Bill Quirke)

Cultivation ridges in the Crinnagh fields. (Bill Quirke)

85

Stone piles in the Crinnagh fields. Stones were piled on rock outcrops to clear the fields and maximise the area available for grazing and cultivation. (Bill Quirke)

more field walls, clear and mossless, are to be seen. The closely cropped sward of grass in these fields shows green against the buff and russet of the surrounding mountain vegetation. In a month or so this ghost landscape will fade again, obscured by the lush growth and engulfing greenness of the mountain grass and bracken fern. But for now we can see that these wild woods and mountains were once populated by people who cleared fields wherever they could find a patch of promising soil with a sunny aspect. With the cleared stones and boulders, they built field walls and cabins in which to live. Sometimes they piled the stones into stacks which still stand like strange monuments in the deserted fields. They dug the thin soil, enriched with leaves and manure and lime, into wide ridges separated by narrow trenches, to grow their crops. Our story concerns these people. Who were they? How did they live? How long did they live here? Where did they go, leaving no account and little memory behind them?

The names of the townlands along the old Kenmare road are hauntingly musical; Cloghfune, Crinnagh, Ferta, Cores, Gortroe, Poulagower, Ullauns – the names seem spoken by wind in heather or mountain streams

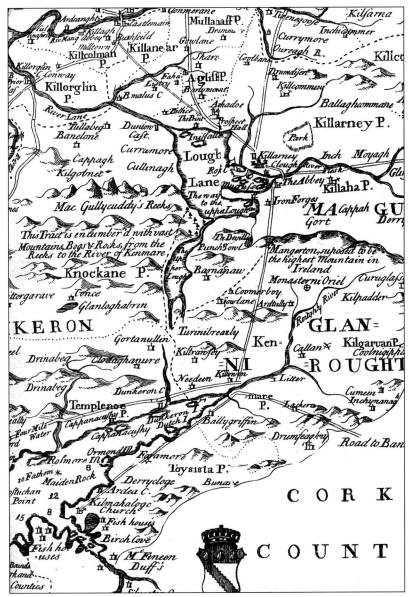

Map of Killarney in 1756 from The ancient and Present State of the County of Kerry *by Charles Smith.*

flowing under peat. The stones and ridges tell us that each of these town-lands was populated, but strangely these names are almost entirely missing from the sparse church and estate records that survive. Records of marriages and baptisms going back to the late eighteenth century are held at Killarney Cathedral. Among the familiar Killarney townland names lie occasional references to an area called 'Glynns', a name unknown and unused today. Close examination of the church archive reveals a few entries which, as well as referring to Glynns, give a townland name as well. For example, we have in 1812 the marriage of Mary Leahy of Cloghfune-Glynns, in 1820 of Margaret Quirke of Glynns-Derrycunihy, in 1825 of Catherine Hurley of Allanes-Glynns, and in 1828 of Mary Connane of Glens-Cores. These records establish that the name Glynns refers to the ten or so mountain townlands which now make up the main south-eastern mountain area of the national park.

Having established the location of the 'Glynns' we can trace the slender thread of name clues further back into the past. Perhaps the earliest clue can be found among the manuscripts preserved in the library of Lambeth Palace

The Old Weir Bridge.
(Isaac Weld 1807)

in England which contain a survey of the forfeited lands of the MacCarthys and the O'Donoghues in the sixteenth century. This document refers to *the Glans of Barenesna which are remote and unaccessable but with much paines in time of feare*. Old maps and references indicate that the area known as the 'Glynns' in the nineteenth century corresponds to the area referred to as 'Barenesnaw' or the 'Glans' or 'Glynns' of 'Barenesnaw' in the sixteenth to eighteenth centuries. Barnasnaw roughly translated from Irish would mean the Gap of the Swimmable Ford or a mountain gap where a river could be crossed on horseback. Before the construction of the Old Weir Bridge the only place where a horse rider could have crossed from the east to the west of the Killarney valley without travelling many miles north or south was at a crossing point that lies between the Eagle's Nest Mountain and the western flank of Torc Mountain. The importance of this crossing point is also indicated by the name of the large townland on its western side which is Glena, translated in the Ordnance Survey Name Books of 1845 as the 'glen of the ford'. This crossing is still used by conservation volunteers who wade across here in dry summers to gain access to the remote western woods of the park. It is my belief that this is the gap of the swimmable ford. I have found no written reference to the name Barnasnaw applying to this precise location; however Thomas Gallwey in his *Lays of the Killarney Lakes*, published in 1871, states that:

> The southern tributary to Loughlin . . . though mentioned in guide-books as the Long-range River, its proper name, now seldom or never used, is Barrnasna, so called from the old name of the Upper Lake, which discharges its overflow through this channel.

I believe that rather than the Upper Lake giving its old name to the river, the river (named from the gap and ford through which it flowed) actually gave its name to the lake above it, and the Upper Lake was indeed referred to as Lough 'Ballenasa', 'Bearnasnow' or 'Varnasnaw' in seventeenth- and eighteenth-century documents. I believe the lake in turn gave its name to the surrounding valleys which were known as the Glynns of Barnasnaw. By the time of the English conquest in the sixteenth century, the area to the east and perhaps to the south of the lake was known as the 'Glans of Barenesna'. By the middle of the eighteenth century the name had been abbreviated in common usage to the 'Glynns' which was used throughout the nineteenth century to be eventually lost from living memory early in this century.

Whether the Killarney mountains were inhabited in the centuries before the Kerry population was devastated by the Tudor conquest is not known. The picture that emerges from the few references to the area of the Glans of Barnasnaw from the sixteenth to the eighteenth centuries, is of a wild place regarded with distaste and some fear by the English settlers. A strong tradition holds that after the destruction of the Abbey of Irrelagh (Muckross Abbey) in 1652 by Cromwellian forces, Franciscan Friars maintained a presence in the mountains until the late eighteenth century when they were free to establish themselves again in the lowlands. M.J. Moriarty wrote in 1954 that in the mid eighteenth century Franciscans:

> had a rough habitation in the Friars' Glen, a bleak and desolate place between the mountains of Torc and Mangerton, and here Brother Donal O'Sullivan wrote his *Ancient History of the Kingdom of Kerry*.

The area between Torc and Mangerton mountains is still known as 'The Friar's Glen'. The Friars were not the only fugitives to take refuge in the Glans of Barnasnaw. Hickson writing in 1874 in her Old Kerry Records refers to the 'passes between Kenmare and Killarney' as one of the areas where in the seventeenth and eighteenth century:

> ...the ousted Irish, and the Anglo-Irish, the descendants of the Englishmen of Plantagenet or Tudor times, became outlaws and robbers on the mountains and unprofitable lands amidst rocks, bogs... looking down and inland upon the rich harvests and herds of their rivals.

The first indication of a settled population in these mountains after the English occupation are in the Kenmare family papers which refer in 1722 to 'several tenants' in 'the Glins' and in 1725 to a James Tuohill, a woodranger in the 'Glins of Barenesnawe'. However, most evidence suggests that the area was virtually unpopulated until the late eighteenth century. In 1756 Thomas Browne, 4th Viscount Kenmare, refers in his private notebook to the:

> Glinns in and about the upper lakes... These which contain many thousand acres, are mostly stupendous craggy mountains, little pasture

on them . . . but on their sides are very large and beautiful woods as thriving as in the Kingdom . . . My father got scarce any rent from them. When I came of age Counsellor Herbert recommended leaving them waste as he thought the immense growth of wood it would occasion would more than pay me for the rents.

In 1756 Charles Smith published his book *The Ancient and Present State of the County of Kerry*. Of these Killarney mountains he writes:

The principle inhabitants of these lofty mountains, except a few woodmen, kept in these forests by the lords of the soil, are great herds of red deer.

The old road to Kenmare where it passes through Ullauns Wood.
(Bill Quirke)

Smith estimates the total population of County Kerry at that time to have been only 51,140 people. The first road from Killarney to Kenmare (the Old Kenmare Road) was built shortly before Smith's visit:

> This was for several years thought impracticable and yet considering its length, and the carrying of it through almost impassable mountains, was at length completed at a small expense, to the great improvement of the country.

The English agriculturalist Arthur Young travelled this road from Kenmare to Killarney in 1777 and mentions no human habitation before Muckross, but comments that "these mountains were not incapable from climate of being applied to useful purposes". Given the sparse population of the county, and the inaccessibility and the marginal nature of the area for agricultural activity, we can hazard a guess that the main settlement of the area began no earlier than the late eighteenth century.

In the early years of the nineteenth century the population of Ireland increased dramatically from an estimated five million in 1800 to between eight and nine million in 1841. This is the most likely period for the establishment of the remoter settlements in the park. The baptism records for 'The Glynns' indicate a very small population prior to 1800 though a significant population already existed in Tomies to the west of Lough Leane. But in the first few decades of the nineteenth century the number of children baptised from the Glynns rapidly increased. So we can begin to construct our picture of these people in the context of Kerry in the late eighteenth and early nineteenth centuries. During this time a succession of adventurous travellers visited the area and left written accounts. Twenty years after Charles Smith's account, a Mr Dunne visited the area. In the midst of romantic descriptions of the landscape, garnished with classical references, he describes an encounter at O'Sullivans cascade in Tomies Wood:

> At some distance from the cascade there are two or three rude cottages, inhabited by a set of hardy mountaineers, who probably subsist by the chase. They generally come down to traffic with strangers, bringing with them nuts, and wild berries; and sometimes cuttings of yew, thorn and oak, for walking sticks.

Cultivation ridges in the remote Glaisín na Marbh *valley. (Bill Quirke)*

A few years later Arthur Young travelled through Ireland and visited Killarney. Young's account gives us some idea of what the 'rude cottages' seen by Dunne in Tomies wood may have looked like:

> The cottages of the Irish which are called cabins, are the most miserable looking hovels that can well be conceived, they generally consist of only one room, mud kneaded with straw is the common material of the walls: these are rarely above seven feet high and not always above five or six; they are about two feet thick and have only a door which lets in light instead of a window and should let the smoke out instead of a chimney but they had rather keep it in . . . The furniture of the cabins is as bad as the architecture; in very many, consisting only of a pot for boiling potatoes, a bit of a table and one or two broken stools, beds are not found universally the family lying on straw equally partook of by cows calves and pigs.

The reasons for the poverty of much of the Irish population at this time are beyond the scope of this chapter, but the means by which the teeming poor fed themselves are central to our story. Potatoes and milk sustained the

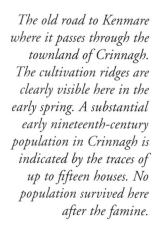

The old road to Kenmare where it passes through the townland of Crinnagh. The cultivation ridges are clearly visible here in the early spring. A substantial early nineteenth-century population in Crinnagh is indicated by the traces of up to fifteen houses. No population survived here after the famine.

population, and these were the only means by which people could produce enough food to live in the mountain areas of the park.

For our next glimpse into the past we travel forward another 25 years to the visit of Isaac Weld in 1800. Weld spent several months in Killarney and wrote the most detailed account we have of the park area at that time. As with Dunne, Weld visited settlements whose ruined cottages and fields are still to be seen. By rowing from Lough Leane up the Long Range river to the Upper Lake he visited an area now known as Tower Wood.

> Along the banks runs an irregular path, on following which nothing can be discerned for half a mile except the river and the woods; but at the end of that distance a wide space suddenly opens, in the centre of which stands a few cottages surrounded by little fields . . . No vestige of human industry appears beyond the precincts of the hamlet; woods and mountains surround it . . . the plough has never left its furrows on this vale; the soil is turned with the spade; and the produce, if more than sufficient for the humble cultivators, is conveyed away on horses, by a craggy path which winds along the borders of the stream.

Though corroborating much of Arthur Young's account, Weld paints a less grim picture of life in the mountains.

> Wild and dreary as the vast region of mountains on the western side of the County of Kerry appears to be, it boasts nevertheless of a numerous and hardy population. The chief occupation of the people is pasturage, and from the milk of their herds a large portion of that excellent butter is produced which is exported from Cork and Limerick to every quarter of the globe. The butter of this country is almost all conveyed to Cork by the peasants who make it, and it is common to meet twenty horses or more in a string on a leading mountain road, each one carrying two casks.

It is hard to imagine how cattle could be supported through the winter in these mountains, but Weld describes how:

> hay for the winter is procured for the most part from the mountains, where it is collected from various little spots on which the grass, from being sheltered by rocks, or from growing on a drier soil, is found to be luxuriant. It is common for a man, in the season, to traverse the side of a mountain with a scythe, and cut the grass perhaps from fifty small patches which when accumulated together does not produce one ton of hay.

As well as the cattle, Weld writes that:

> Immense herds of goats are likewise fed in these mountains, whose milk is chiefly used by the peasants for their domestic purposes." And for crops "the inhabitants are satisfied with tilling small patches near their dwellings, sufficient to produce some oats or potatoes, which with milk constitute their chief food." Fuel according to Weld "is abundant throughout the mountains, it consists of turf or peat, furze and heath, which last commonly attains the height of six feet.

Despite living at subsistence level, the picture that emerges from contemporary accounts of these mountain dwellers is not a picture of a desperate or degraded people. Isaac Weld describes a well-developed system of communal co-operation:

> It is usual for many different families to form a partnership and make a joint concern of their several farms . . . It saves the labour and expense

The Ferta fields. This townland had a population of ten people in 1841 and became depopulated during the famine years.
(Bill Quirke)

of multiplied superintendence; it excites attention to the general interest; and prevents disputes that would otherwise arise concerning boundaries . . . Each man in proportion to the computed extent of his land is permitted to maintain a certain number of cattle; and in many instances where the parties have confidence in each other, they make a joint stock both of their kine and their produce.

Formal education was not neglected. Weld observed:

Amidst some of the wildest mountains of Kerry I have met with English schools, and have seen multitudes of children seated round the humble residence of their instructor, with their books, pens and inks, where rocks have supplied the place of desks and benches.

The growing of potatoes required little attention except for the spring planting and the harvest. So these now deserted mountains and woods must have been criss-crossed with paths worn by the visiting, courting, helping and gossiping of the community. In winter with high winds and heavy rain, these people lived much of the time literally in the clouds. During the long winter nights, with the potatoes harvested and the turf stacked by the cabins, they sat around their fires, playing music, talking, singing and telling stories. *The love of dancing and music are almost universal amongst them*, wrote Arthur Young of the Kerry mountain people. And Cecil Woodham-Smith writing of that time says,

> Groups of neighbours gathered for dancing to the fiddle, indoors in the winter, in summer at the crossroads, wakes, with liberal potations of poteen, were social occasions; and crowds gaily travelled immense distances to attend markets, fairs and, above all, races.

> If there be a market to attend, a fair or a funeral, a horse race, a fight or a wedding, all else is neglected and forgotten,

wrote George Nicholls of Ireland at that time.

Wakes and races certainly provided amusement for the mountain people of Killarney and perhaps we can see them mingling in the crowds when Thackeray paid his visit to the Killarney races. William Makepeace Thackeray opens another window for us on Killarney's past. It was 1842 and:

> the sun lighted up the whole (race) course and the lakes with amazing brightness, though behind the former lay a huge rack of the darkest clouds against which the cornfields and meadows shone in the brightest green and gold, and a row of white tents was quite dazzling. There was a brightness and intelligence about this immense Irish crowd, which I don't remember having seen in an English one. The women in their blue cloaks, with red smiling faces peering from one end, and bare feet from the other, had seated themselves in all sorts of pretty attitudes of cheerful contemplation; and the men, who are accustomed to lie about, were doing so now with all their might – sprawling on the banks with as much ease and variety as club-room loungers on their soft cushions, – or squatted leisurely among the green potatoes. The sight of so much happy laziness did one good to look on . . . The tents were long humble booths stretched on hoops each with its humble streamer or ensign without, and containing, of course, articles of refreshment within. But Father Matthew has been busy among the publicans, and the consequence is,

that the poor fellows are now condemned for the most part to sell "tay" in place of whiskey; for the concoction of which beverage, huge cauldrons were smoking in front of each hut door, in round graves dug for the purpose and piled up with black smoking sods. Behind this camp were the carts of the poor people, which were not allowed to penetrate into the quarter where the quality cars stood. And a little way from the huts again, you might see (for you could scarcely hear) certain pipers executing their melodies and inviting people to dance.

We take leave of the early years of the last century and move on to the last days of the inhabitants of the Killarney mountains. But before we go, Isaac Weld sums up for us much of the happiness of this time and the grim seeds of a disaster beyond the imaginings of the visiting Dublin man or the people he describes:

They marry at a very early age, the men commonly at eighteen, the females much sooner; and it is no rare occurrence to behold four generations together in health and vigour. The inducements to marriage are numerous; the impediments few. The extent of the mountain-farms being, in general, great, they admit of a division proportionate to the increase of the people. A habitation for the new married couple is built at a trifling expense. Stones suitable for the purpose abound in every place; and it requires little skill to heap them together in form of a wall, and plaster them with clay; the heath provides material for the thatch. A plot of ground is readily converted into a potato garden; and its never failing produce is generally more than adequate to the wants of the little family.

Thackeray's account in 1842 shows us the country on the very brink of the disaster. His journey from Cork to Bantry could as well describe the Killarney mountain area:

The ride is desolate, bare and yet beautiful . . . There was only one wretched village along the road, but no lack of population; ragged people who issued from their cabins as the coach passed, or were sitting by the wayside . . . The wretchedness of them (the cabins) is quite painful to look at; many potato gardens were half dug up, and it is only the first week in August, near three months before the potato is ripe and at full growth and the winter still six months away." "The people . . . look for the most part healthy enough; especially the small children, those who can scarcely totter, and are sitting shading their eyes at the door, and leaving the unfinished dirt pie to shout as the coach passes by are as healthy a looking race as one will often see. Nor can anyone pass through the land without being touched by the extreme love of children among the people; they swarm everywhere, and the whole country rings with cries of affection towards the children, with the songs of young ragged nurses dandling babies in their knees, and warnings of mothers to Patsy to come out of the mud, or Nory to get off the pigs back."

Seven years later Mr Trench, a landlord's agent in Kenmare, was to write:

> . . . they died on the roads, and they died in the fields, they died in the mountains and they died in the glens, they died at the relief works, and they died in their houses; so that the little streets or villages were left almost without inhabitants; and at least some few, despairing of help in the country, crawled into the town and died at the doors of the residents and outside the union walls. Some were buried underground, and some were left unburied in the mountains where they died, there being no one able to bury them.

Local tradition (see Chapter 7) indicates that the depopulation of the Killarney mountains began with evictions well before the Great Famine and though I have found no written record of such evictions, there is some evidence of possible evictions at this time. Tradition holds that evictions took place in the village of Crinnagh. Though the remains of fifteen houses can be found in this townland and eleven houses are shown on the 1841 map, the 1841 census records only one house and a population of five in Crinnagh.

There can be little doubt that for many of the mountain people the end came in the years of the Great Famine from 1846 to 1849. Rumours of the approaching disaster must have reached the mountains from Killarney town. August 1845 produced the first reports of 'a blight of unusual character' appearing in the potato crops in Britain. By September it was reported in Ireland:

We stop the press with very great regret to announce that the potato murrain (blight) has unequivocally declared itself in Ireland. The crops about Dublin are suddenly perishing . . . where will Ireland be in the event of a universal potato rot?"

A partial failure of the crop in 1845 may have left the mountain people unscathed, but in 1846 the failure of the potato crop was universal. On 7 August, Father Matthew wrote:

On the 27th of last month I passed from Cork to Dublin and this doomed plant bloomed in all the luxuriance of an abundant harvest. Returning on the third instant I beheld with sorrow one wide waste of putrefying vegetation. In many places the wretched people were seated on the fences of their decaying gardens, wringing their hands and wailing bitterly the destruction that had left them foodless.

Throughout the country the stench from the rotting potatoes was *intolerable*. Another wrote *the fields in Kerry look as if fire had passed over them.* And so the blight reached the little potato fields of the mountain people of Killarney. Many of the potato ridges in the national park are steep sided and sharp in outline, clear evidence that they were never harvested. Surrounded as they were by woodlands and wild mountains, the universe of the mountain people must have remained strangely and cruelly normal compared with the lowlands. With no food reserves and living already at the edge of subsistence, events must now have moved rapidly. We will never know what most of them did. Killarney town was within easy reach, so perhaps whole families with their old people and children moved down to the town, where the population was swelling rapidly with desperate people from the surrounding countryside. More likely many of them remained in the mountains for at least a few months while visiting the town or Muckross village to seek food. The following winter of 1846–47 was, *the most severe in living memory.* Woodham-Smith describes the conditions:

Snow fell early in November, frost was continuous, icy gales blew perfect hurricanes of snow, hail and sleet with a force unknown since the famous great wind of 1839; roads were impassable and transport was brought to a standstill.

In Killarney town it is said that construction work on the new cathedral ceased and the unfinished building was used to shelter the victims of starvation and pestilence. In February 1847 there was only one soup kitchen for 10,000 persons in Killarney town. Two years later out of a population of 30,000 people in the Kenmare area to the south of the mountains, over 5,000 had died. Many of the mountain people, particularly the old and the children, must have died that winter or over the next few years of the Great Famine, when starvation was assisted by epidemics of cholera, typhoid and dysentery. The 1841 census gives a population of almost 100 for the townlands of the Glynns, though as we will see there is evidence that this is probably an underestimate. Ten years later the population had been almost halved.

What happened to those that left the mountains and lived is not known, but they probably joined the anonymous mass of millions of starving and utterly destitute Irish, fleeing the land and the country. Those who made it to a new land and survived were the lucky ones. Some may have been among the thousands that died on the infamous 'coffin ships' that carried emigrants to America. Some may have survived their journey but died at their port of arrival and may lie buried in mass graves such as the one on Grosse Île in Canada marked by a monument inscribed:

> In this secluded spot lie the mortal remains of 5,294 persons who, flying from the pestilence and famine in Ireland in the year 1847 found in America but a grave.

As far west as California, if you visit the cemeteries in the old Spanish Missions you will find the graves of many young Irish people who made it so far but died of disease during the early 1850s. Some may have survived, and there may well be people living in the United States, Canada, Australia, Britain or even Killarney, whose great grandparents were born in the tiny cabins, now roofless and cushioned in moss in the woods and mountains of Killarney National Park.

T.J. Barrington sums up the Great Famine in Ireland:

> In the early 1840's over two million people – one quarter of the population – were living on the verge of destitution. What the famine did

was to destroy these people – killing half of them by hunger and disease and sending the rest – starving, half naked, fever ridden, destitute, panic stricken, embittered – across the Atlantic.

So this incomplete jigsaw puzzle picture is the best we can do to lift the veil that covers the fate of the pre-famine inhabitants of the Killarney mountains. Estimating the population of the mountains before the evictions and the famine is also fraught with difficulty. Neither the 1841 census nor the 1841 ordnance survey map gives us a complete picture of the population and house numbers at that time. Townlands with no houses shown on the map may have houses and inhabitants documented by the census, and conversely in some townlands several houses are shown on the map where few are documented by the census.

The destruction and scattering of the mountain people seems to have left little trace in the folk memory of the area. The closest surviving neighbours to the mountain people were in Muckross village. Many of the Muckross people were employees of the landlord at Muckross House, and as such were probably shielded from the fate which befell the inhabitants of the mountains. It is likely that the mountain people still spoke Irish while the Muckross folk spoke English. The reason may also be that some memories are too unpleasant to be passed on to one's children. Within a few years of the famine, in 1853, the new railway line to Killarney was opened, and already seven hotels were catering for the rising tide of tourists. It was easier to forget.

The population that survived in the mountains after the devastating years of eviction and famine now entered a period of steady and eventually terminal decline, revealed in the ten-yearly censuses. From a figure of 105 people in all the mountain townlands in 1851, the population dropped to 47 in 1901. Griffith's valuation in 1852 shows that after the famine a large proportion of the population consisted of caretakers and their families. One by one the townlands became depopulated. Nobody remained in Cloghfune, Crinnagh or Ferta after the famine; Cores was empty by 1861; Ullauns, Gortroe and Poulagower were abandoned by 1871. In townlands where a population survived into the late nineteenth century, the house ruins are more substantial. In Doogary and Cullinagh, the house ruins have fire places and chimneys. The names of these last families survive in the memories of people like Paddy Cremin who farmed the land adjoining the national park

A lone holly on a stone pile in the Crinnagh fields. (Bill Quirke)

at Tomies, like his father and grandfather before him (see Chapter 7). Paddy tells that the Sullivans of Doogary, at the north-west corner of the Upper Lake, moved out in 1895. Dan Sullivan moved to Cullinagh, south of Tomies Wood, while his brothers moved to Kilgarvan or America. Cullinagh was abandoned in 1901 after the Breen and Sullivan families had moved out to Beaufort and Tomies East. Paddy Cremin recalls his parents describing how once a month Mrs Sullivan used to travel out by pony from Cullinagh through Tomies Wood to Killarney. The Vincent family, who bought the Muckross estate from the Herberts, purchased farms for several of their tenants on better land outside the national park area. Thus the Ferris family from Tomies Wood were moved to Killorglin in 1901, and Paddy Cremin's great uncle Tim Cremin was moved from Tomies Wood to Torc around 1919, where he and his family were given employment on the Muckross estate. Tim Cremin's grandson, Timmy Joe Cremin, works at Muckross for Killarney National Park.

Even until recent times a small twilight population of caretakers and gamekeepers lived on in the area of the present park. Dan Donoghue, the

The ruin of 'Doty' Donoghue's cottage at Derrycunihy. (Bill Quirke)

gamekeeper, left his remote house at Incheens in the south of the park around 1964. In the 1970s 'Doty' Donoghue left the cottage whose ruin can still be seen beside the site of the old 'Queen's Cottage' at Derrycunihy. On the remote and beautiful shore of Glena Bay on the Lower Lake, behind the ruins of Glena cottage, a derelict caretaker's cottage can still be seen, surrounded by the oakwoods and now nearly lost in rhododendron. Here Dan Doyle lived with his wife and children. The sixteen Doyle children were born in this cottage, and according to Paddy Cremin, the nurse who delivered them travelled in by boat across the 'back channel' from Dinis Island. Mrs Doyle, on her trips into town, would row across the back channel taking some of her children and towing the pony behind the boat. On the Dinis side she would hitch the pony to the trap (cart) which was kept there and drive the seven miles into town. The Doyles moved out in the early 1950s. Sheila and Mary Kelliher were the last people to live in the remoter areas of the national park. Beyond the reach of the electricity supplies, and cut off from the public road whenever the lake level was high, they provided a warm welcome for visitors to Dinis cottage until they moved out in 1985.

Now that they are gone, these last gamekeepers and caretakers seem to have been like lighthouse keepers in an empty ocean. After the Great Famine the population faded and the mountains and woods were left to the deer. The thatches of the deserted cabins soon collapsed, leaving the walls to the moss and weather. While in other areas a new less numerous generation of farmers amalgamated fields, fenced the land, and used the stones for their own purposes, in Killarney the stones remained where they were piled, and the unharvested ridges remained undug. And so we are left with one of the least disturbed nineteenth-century landscapes in Ireland; a reminder of a hardy people, of a tragedy which is still experienced by many of the world's poor, and of events which utterly changed the history both of Ireland and of the countries to which these people fled.

Postscript

Most of the story recounted in this chapter was played out along the 'old Kenmare road'. In the few years since this chapter was written the old road has probably seen more changes than it had since the last inhabitants left. In 1993 2.5 km of the old road through the townland of Crinnagh was resurfaced. Increasing numbers of walkers have sought out the old road, and sections of the route overgrown by bog have had paths and boardwalks constructed to facilitate walkers and reduce damage to the mountain environment. A 1 km square block of mountain adjoining the old road, including the old fields of Ferta, has been fenced to contain cattle for an experiment on the regeneration of mountain vegetation. A major development of holiday houses on private land has entered the great wide view of apparently wild and empty country from the hill of Knockreer. As the main purpose of this chapter is to describe events in the past rather than the park as it is at present, the text can be left stand, though some of the descriptions of the 'present' have already joined the rest of the chapter in the realm of history.

Chapter 7

MUCKROSS: THE VIEW FROM DOWNSTAIRS.
SOME ORAL TRADITIONS AND SOCIAL HISTORY

Bairbre Ní Fhloinn

In recent years, Killarney National Park has grown considerably in size, and has expanded its boundaries to include much of the old Kenmare Estate. Originally, however, Killarney National Park consisted of a smaller area of land which had previously constituted the old Muckross Estate. The history of the Muckross Estate need not concern us too much here, as it has been dealt with elsewhere in this book. Suffice it to say that the estate had belonged to a succession of private owners, or landlords, until the year 1932, when what remained of the estate was presented as a gift to the people of Ireland by the Vincent family, who then owned it. Thus the nucleus of the present-day park came into being.

As part of the activities organised to commemorate the fiftieth anniversary of this event, I was asked to collect the folklore of the Muckross Estate from oral tradition, while there were still people alive who could remember the old dispensation. This I did, in the winter and spring of 1982–83, basing my work on the idea of folklore as the history that never got into the history books – the history of the ordinary people as opposed to the history of the 'Great Men and Great Events'. Most of the previous work on the history of Muckross had been based on official, conventional sources and on the written record. This work, important as it was, could be said to represent only the bones of the story. The purpose of my work at Muckross was to try to put some flesh on the bones and to see what everyday life was like for the people living and working on the estate in its later years. For this reason, I started off with a fairly wide brief, encompassing most aspects of life on the estate

* See note at end of chapter for information on source materials, etc.

The Muckross Estate, like most large landlords' estates, was made up of both the demesne and the surrounding land. The demesne consisted of the parkland, gardens, etc., immediately surrounding the Big House, and this part of the estate was surrounded by a high wall. Predictably, this wall seems to have caused a certain amount of resentment among the people. For example Mrs Mary O'Connor, formerly of Gearhameen, told me how her grand-mother told her that the women of that area were forced to carry stones on their backs for the building of the wall around Lord Brandon's Cottage, which was on the estate. Similarly, Mrs Joan Lyne of Torc, from whom I recorded quite an amount of information, and who has sadly since died, described to me how her father worked on the building of part of the demesne wall near Muckross for ten old pennies per day. Her remark about the wall was, *'Thank God I lived to see it knocked'*. The Muckross Estate proper, however, consisted of all the land belonging to the landlord, amounting to some 14,000 acres at the beginning of the twentieth century. This land was let to tenant-farmers, who in turn often sub-let their holdings. It is worth mentioning here that the Muckross Estate was mostly mountain, with mere pockets of cultivation here and there, notably around the area of Muckross itself and around Tomies. Apart from that, the land tends to be very rugged and very beautiful, but very difficult to make a living on – in other words, not the type of landscape to lend itself to a high density of population.

The Herberts

Having got my bearings in Muckross in a geographical sense, it did not take me very long to learn that the people of Muckross were not one homogen-ous, uniform mass. On the contrary, there were clearly defined social and occupational groups to be found in Muckross as elsewhere, the obvious dif-ference between landlord and tenant being only the beginning of the story. The Muckross Estate was originally owned by the McCarthys, one of the great native landowning families of Kerry. By means of a marriage between the McCarthys and the Herberts, the Muckross lands passed into the hands of the Herberts around the beginning of the eighteenth century. The Herberts were originally from Monmouthshire in Wales, although they had been in Ireland since the late sixteenth century. As virtually no oral tradition now exists about the McCarthys in Muckross, we must take the Herberts as our starting point for traditions about the owners of Muckross.

The Herberts emerge in a generally benign light in modern-day tradition, for the most part. They gave presents to their workers at Christmas and are remembered as having taken good care of the poor. Similarly, whenever I asked about evictions in the area, I was invariably told that the Herberts were never notorious for evicting people, but that a reputation for evictions did attach to the landlords on the neighbouring Kenmare Estate, part of which is now included in the national park. This is interesting in that the Kenmares were Catholic and they were, apparently, more closely identified with the old Gaelic order in the past than were the Herberts. It should also be noted that the Kenmares are remembered less favourably than the Herberts not only by former Muckross tenants, but also by some former Kenmare tenants with whom I spoke.

The Herberts were certainly not regarded as angels by their tenantry, however. One of my informants referred to *'old Herbert'* as *'a limb of the devil'* and, although she didn't specify which of the Herberts she had in mind, her general attitude was clear enough! Several anecdotes are told which reflect far from favourably on the Herberts, and these include occasional stories of evictions. According to tradition, several families were evicted by the Herberts in the area of the old Killarney-Kenmare road. It was said that the evictions were carried out in order to create a deer park, although it should be noted that the historical record does not bear this out. Nonetheless, the oral traditions about the evictions are worth recording, and have their own significance as an indicator of popular attitudes and perceptions. The old Killarney-Kenmare road, which is now part of the Kerry Way walking route, was in use until the construction of the new road about 1824. It ran between Mangerton Mountain and Torc Mountain, and past the villages of Ferta and Crinnagh. It was from these two villages that the families are said to have been evicted. The story goes that, in the case of Crinnagh, the people were driven out rather than evicted. Not having an excuse to evict, the Herberts are said to have employed a man to go to Crinnagh and to stay there all night, playing the one note on his concertina! It is not clear how many nights this was continued, but the desired effect was achieved and the people eventually left, whether from fear or frustration, according to Danny Cronin of

Muckross: *'I'm only talking now from what I was told by some of the old fellows. They shifted them out to make room for deer'.*

Ferta is situated in a place known as the Friars' Glen, because the friars from Muckross Abbey are said to have taken refuge there, after they were driven out of the Abbey. Paudie Cremin, a retired gamekeeper from Tomies, told me the story of the evictions:

When the Herberts went about removing the tenants out of this place, to leave it all together as a deer-forest, it was said they had to get some excuse to evict a tenant – either he didn't pay his rent, or he wasn't farming, or he had to commit some offence before they could make a case for it. So it was said that the Herberts this time planted conifers, and the trees they planted were larch, in the Friars' Glen. And they just planted the young trees and, at that time, there was a goat kept on every farm and the purpose was, if the goats would eat the young trees, then they had a case. The goats ate them, and they had an excuse. There's an odd couple of them – but they're very old – there's a couple of them left all the time, of the larch trees in the Friars' Glen. No other purpose. In all this area, there is no other larch or pine or spruce or what-have-you – only in the Friars' Glen.

Paudie Cremin of Tomies. (B. Ní Fhloinn, Department of Irish Folklore, University College Dublin)

In the 1841–42 edition of the Ordnance Survey map of the area, there are houses marked in both Crinnagh and Ferta. In the 1895 edition of the map, there is no sign of these houses. The 1841 census returns record one inhabited house and five people living in Crinnagh, with two inhabited houses and ten people living in Ferta. Both houses and people have disappeared from both townlands in the 1851 census. In view of this, it is of course possible that the two townlands were, in fact, depopulated at the time as a result of famine, or for other reasons (see chapter 6).

Other stories about the Herberts include the following, told by Danny Cronin of Muckross. Danny, it should be said, is a mine of information on every aspect of the history and folklore of the Muckross Estate.

> Of course, at one time, I was told that the horses, the common carts, the drivers wouldn't be left up on them. They had to walk by the horse's head. Oh yes, they had to walk by the horse's head until, one time, there was an old Mulligan here, a carter, and old Herbert caught him up on the horse, sitting on the horse. And he reprimanded him anyway and Mulligan said to him, 'The ship that can't carry her captain should never leave her port!'. That shut him up! And it may be just a yarn but I often heard the old men talking about it anyway.

Another story tells how some workmen found a large sum of money on the site of an old carpenter's workshop one day while working in the demesne. They handed it all up to Herbert, and it is said that it was with this money that Herbert paid the Butlers, a family of stonemasons from Killorglin, for their work in building the Muckross church, the front lodge and entrance to Muckross House and the bridge on the front drive. When Herbert was asked if he had rewarded the men for handing up the money, his reply was reported to have been, *'They have themselves well paid'*, implying that the men had helped themselves to some of it before handing it up. One of the workmen involved in this episode was an ancestor of Danny Cronin, who told me the story.

In the manuscript collection of the Department of Irish Folklore in University College Dublin (formerly the Irish Folklore Commission), there are also some critical references to the Herberts. Some of these references describe how Minor Herbert once insulted a local

Danny Cronin of Muckross. (B. Ní Fhloinn, Department of Irish Folklore, University College Dublin)

111

poet, Séamus Crón Ó Súilleabháin, in return for which the poet wrote a very bitter satirical poem about Herbert.

Whether these derogatory stories are strictly true or not is hardly the point. What is significant is that they reflect a certain attitude on the part of the people and, predictably, a great deal of hidden resentment, no matter how good relations might appear to have been on the surface. This situation is hardly to be wondered at when we remember that the Herberts were, after all, apart from the people in religion, in language and in political aspirations.

In 1889, the Herberts left Muckross, and the house and estate had a succession of different owners for the following twenty years or so. In 1910, however, events took a major change when William Bowers Bourn, a Californian millionaire, bought the house and estate as a wedding-present for his daughter, Maud, and son-in-law, Arthur Vincent. I talked to Billy Vincent, son of Maud and Arthur Vincent, about his early memories of Muckross and his impressions of it. He described to me the poverty which he remembered seeing around Muckross as a child, and how shocked their visiting American friends used to be at the sight of the local children going barefoot in both winter and summer. The Vincents were certainly very popular as employers and as landlords although, of course, the number of tenants on the estate in their time was only a fraction of what it had been in the Herberts' time. This was still before the days of trade unions in Muckross, however, and Danny Cronin remembers how, when he started working in Muckross as a young lad, he was told by an older man not to work too far away from his coat – the ominous implications being obvious! The Vincents continued the Herberts' custom of giving presents to the estate workers at Christmas. This usually consisted of beef or venison, and every man and boy got a new woollen cardigan of a particular design.

Workers and Tenants

Moving down the social pyramid, we come to the workers and tenants of Muckross who, of course, made up the bulk of the people living on the estate. Starting with the estate workers, it is interesting to note that the upper levels of staff were often occupied by people from England or Scotland, who were brought in specially for the job by the Herberts, and later by the

Bridge on the front drive of Muckross House which was funded from a cache of money found in the demesne, according to Danny Cronin of Muckross. (B. Ní Fhloinn, Department of Irish Folklore, University College Dublin)

113

Vincents. Such people included butlers, housekeepers, head gamekeepers, farmyard managers, etc. Perhaps it was felt that the local people did not have the training or experience required to fill these important positions. Again, Danny Cronin is a rich source of detail here.

In Muckross House itself, there was a large retinue of household staff operating beneath the butler, the housekeeper and the cook. These included the footmen, the hall boy, the odd man, the cook, kitchen maids, scullery maids, housemaids, etc., with the butler and the footmen attired in special livery-type uniform. In the Vincents' time, there were approximately twenty-two people working in the house in all. Mention should also be made of the special connection between Muckross House and the various Doody families living on the estate. At one stage, when the Vincents were in Muckross, Mick Doody was the head gardener, Willy Doody worked in the greenhouses, Jack Doody worked in the main gatehouse, Annie Doody was a nursemaid, Nellie Doody was a kitchen maid and cook, Dempsey Doody was a gamekeeper, Kitty Doody was a housemaid, Conny Doody was a groom, Jackie Doody worked in the farmyard, Sheila Doody was a kitchen maid and Denis Doody worked in the rock garden. The various Doody families from which they all came were, apparently, related to each other.

The household staff had their own domestic routine, and much of the work they had to do clearly reflects the fact that these were the days of cheap labour, and before the labour-saving gadgets of today. Many of the chores involved hard work and painstaking thoroughness. For example, the floors were polished with real beeswax, as Danny Cronin tells us:

> They used polish with beeswax – buy the beeswax and melt it down. 'Twas put in jars and put into hot water and melted down. They wouldn't mix it with anything. It was put on with cloths then and polished. It might be done maybe once a week. And then there were polishers – they had a heavy lead weight that was pushed over it (the floor), with a cloth around the weight. It was a brush, and they'd wrap a cloth around it – there was a lead weight in the brush, a lump of lead.

Billy Vincent told me something of the lighting arrangements in Muckross House when he lived there, including the curious fitting, for two candles, beside the bed, so that you could read in comfort! From the 'down-

stairs' point of view, the cleaning and care of the lighting utensils alone
sounds like a full day's work. Danny Cronin tells us:

> Lighting was all oil lamps, and petrol in the end of the time. These
> lamps used be lit in the evening. They had the lamp-room there. There
> was a room in the basement there that was used – you'd see maybe
> twenty or thirty of these lamps – they'd be lit maybe an hour before-
> hand, before darkness, because these lamps, they used to make a lot of
> noise, kind of a roar until they'd heat up, and they'd have to be adjust-
> ed then.

Incidentally, another Doody, Mike, looked after the lamps.

Inside and outside the house, there were a number of tradesmen and
craftsmen employed full-time on the estate. There were two carpenters,
one for inside work and one for outside work, the latter being Danny
Cronin's father. Danny's father's work included making and repairing
farm-carts and gates, and looking after the estate cottages, etc. Meanwhile,
the 'inside' carpenter was kept occupied repairing furniture, putting in
glass, repairing locks, door-fastenings and so on. The carpenters usually
had an apprentice working with them, the apprentice being Danny for a
number of years.

As well as the craftsmen and tradesmen, there were gardeners required
to keep the extensive gardens in trim, many of them newly laid-out by the
Vincents. Tim Cremin of Torc told me how his father worked as a gardener in the large vegetable garden at Muckross. When he started there, he
worked a six-day week, from eight in the morning until six in the evening,
with no holidays. His weekly wage was one pound, four shillings and eight
pence.

It is worth mentioning that there does not seem to have been any distinction between the different types of workers on the estate. Domestic staff,
farmyard workers, gamekeepers, etc., all appear to have mixed quite freely.
There seems to have been no greater status attached to any one kind of work
than to another, and no particular hierarchy or pecking order among the
workers.

With the exception of the 'imported' staff, whom I've already mentioned,
the people who worked on the Muckross Estate were practically all local

Estate workers house in Muckross. (Bill Quirke)

people, with the bulk of them coming from the estate itself. For some of these full-time workers, special houses were built by the Herberts. There were 25 to 30 of these houses in all, most of which are still lived in today and can be seen along the roads around Muckross. Approximately six of these houses were built about 1874, and these appear to be of Welsh design. The other houses are older, and at least half-a-dozen were originally thatched. This half-a-dozen also show signs of their age in the construction of their walls, in the fact that local Mangerton slate was at one stage used in their roofing, and in the fact that they contained interior turf-partitions at one time, according to Danny Cronin. Danny saw these turf walls in some of the houses before they were removed, and describes them thus: *'It was wooden uprights and the infilling was sods of turf, and lath and plaster then on each side'.*

As well as a rent-free house, other entitlements of workers on the estate included the free grazing of one animal on the estate, free turf, free kindling, a free number of potato drills on the estate, a quarter or an eighth of an acre with their house and – in the Vincents' time, at least – a daily allowance of free milk.

116

Farming

As well as the estate workers, there were the ordinary tenant-farmers of the estate. Unlike the large tenant-farmers, who were comparatively few and far between, most of the tenants lived on small-holdings of land. Their principal – and often their only – connection with the Big House was that they paid their rent to it. According to census returns of the period, there were approximately 1,250 people living on the Muckross Estate at the beginning of the 1850s. When the Vincents took over Muckross in 1910, there were only about 40 or 50 tenants left on the estate, most of the other tenants having bought out their land under the various Land Acts from the 1870s on. One of the remaining tenants in 1910 was Paudie Cremin's father, who farmed 45 acres of land in Tomies, near the Gap of Dunloe. Paudie's great-grandfather had originally come to Tomies from the Barleymount area, because he had the possibility of getting a bigger farm of land in Tomies, on the Muckross Estate. Paudie has described in detail the type of mixed farming practiced by himself, his father and his grandfather, on their comfortable-sized holding. Cattle and butter were the main sources of income. Seven or eight milking cows were usually kept, and their calves were reared until they were two-year-olds. The rent was due to be paid in the autumn of the year, and the cattle were sold in September or October in order to pay it. In summertime, butter was taken into Killarney once a week to be sold. As was the case generally, the woman of the house kept the butter money, and much of this usually went on household expenses. The Cremins did not keep sheep, because they had no grazing rights on the mountain, possibly as a result of their comparatively late arrival in the area. Two pigs were usually bought in April. In November, one of these was killed for their own consumption, while the other one was sold to pay for the keep of the first one.

Hens and ducks were kept for their eggs. When the eggs were sold, the egg money, like the butter money, was kept by the woman of the house. Geese and turkeys were also fattened, for the Christmas market. Potatoes, oats and grass were the principal crops, and they were grown in rotation every year. Tomies produce had a good reputation locally, and some potatoes and oats were usually sold in the spring. A working horse was also kept by the Cremins, and was often used as part of a system of co-operative labour in the area, as Paudie has described to me.

The principal large pieces of equipment used on the farm in Paudie Cremin's young days were the plough, the harrow, the roller and, later, the mowing machine. Sometimes, ploughs, harrows and rollers were held in partnership between different farms. A donkey or a jennet, and a donkey-cart, were usually kept for light work. Fuel consisted of timber and turf. The only difference in Paudie's grandfather's time was that the cultivation work would have been done with a spade, rather than with the implements mentioned above. As Paudie said:

> It was the same thing you did, year-in, year-out. There was very little change. The time came to buy the young pig or the *banbh*, and time came to sell your produce, the potatoes or the oats, the selling of the cattle – they came around the same time every year.

Other Income Sources

The Cremins never supplemented their income by working for the estate. Their relationship with the Big House was confined almost completely to paying their rent to it. Also of interest is the fact that fishing played little or no part in the traditional economy of the tenants. This was, of course, because the fishing rights belonged to the landlord and any fishing that was done was, in theory at least, for the landlord. Needless to say, however, tenants often poached the lake for salmon and trout.

There were, of course, other means of supplementing one's income, such as the various woodland industries, which have now disappeared without trace. Danny Cronin tells us:

> Another thing that's completely gone now is the hoops. There were families here of hoop-splitters, that used split the hazel and sally wattles to make hoops for barrels. They'd earn a living at that. They had a special ring-tool they used drive down through the sally wattle or hazel wattle to split it. Because with all the old barrels, there was no metal hoops in those only wooden hoops. These split wattles were tied in bundles then, and they were tied up with dogwood or gadwood, and this gadwood was split again and passed through the hot embers of a fire, and that used toughen it. And they were tied up with that, and you could actually knot this thing. It's a kind of thorn – there's a few places it's

growing here, out on the Rough Island, and there's more of it down near Torc Boathouse. I believe it was commonly grown for that around various parts of the estate. A few times, I saw these yokes they used split the hoops with. There wasn't any name for them, they were just only a ring with four crossed knives in it. They were driven onto the end of the wattle, and they split it into four.

Another source of supplementary income for the people living around Killarney – and one which was not shared by people in most other parts of the country – was tourism. Killarney might be a busy tourist centre today but, by all accounts, things were equally hectic in days gone by. There seems to have been a particular increase in the numbers of tourists coming to Killarney after the First World War, possibly because of improved communications, etc. One of the most popular trips at that time was the round trip through the Gap of Dunloe. This involved taking a jaunting car as far as the Gap, travelling on pony through the Gap and on to Gearhameen on the shore of the Upper Lake, and travelling back to Killarney by boat. Jack O'Shea of Muckross, now sadly

Michael O'Connor of Gearhameen. (B. Ní Fhloinn, Department of Irish Folklore, University College Dublin)

no longer with us, worked as a boatman for years on the lakes. When he was young, there were, he said, over 300 boatmen on the lakes, many of them working on the last stage of the Gap of Dunloe round trip. Today, there are possibly twenty boatmen working on the lakes, and a smaller proportion of visitors now do the round trip. Arbutus Cottage, in the Gap, with its beautiful hand-carved wooden souvenirs, is closed down, and the *poitín* sellers, who used to ply their trade with the tourists, are no longer.

The Irish Language

The need to communicate with the visitors almost certainly hastened the disappearance of the Irish language from Muckross. Mrs Joan Lyne was of the firm and stated belief that the immediate Muckross area was 'all English' because of the tourists – and she was probably quite right. It seems probable that the area around the Upper Lake, and the part of Mangerton that touched on the estate, were the last places on the estate where Irish was spoken. For example, Mrs Mary O'Connor, formerly of Gearhameen on the Upper Lake remembers her grandfather speaking Irish, and there also seems to be a preponderance of untranslated Irish placenames in that area.

Social Life

Lest it might seem that it was all work and no play for the people of Muckross, it should be said that they also had a vigorous social life. On Sunday evenings in summertime, dancing was held on a platform specially erected for the purpose. This took place on the Fair Green, originally, beside the present Muckross post office, and later in the Football Field or Bog Field, beside the present Muckross House farmyard. Kerry sets were danced and the music was usually provided by a local accordion player. The dancing continued until darkness fell. Then there was the clubhouse, which was organised by Arthur Vincent. It was originally an estate worker's house, and was situated near the farmyard. It is now a dwelling house again. The men could meet here at night, and play cards, or listen to the gramophone which was provided, or read the daily paper which was also supplied. Danny Cronin's comment on the club-house was: *It wound up being known as the House of Lords, because it was only all old fellows used go there!'* It is also worth noting that the clubhouse was frequented not only by the estate workers, but by men in the locality generally.

Beside the clubhouse, there was a bowling green, which brings to mind the cricket teams organised by some landlords amongst their tenants in other parts of the country. Of course, Gaelic football was also played in Muckross, originally in the football field referred to above. Muckross even had its own football team at one stage in the 1930s. Regattas and boat races on the lakes were also very much a feature of life for the people of Muckross and, indeed, continue to be so today.

Probably the most commonly played game in Muckross, however, was pitching. Basically, this game involved throwing pennies as near as possible to a marking stone, known as the Jack. Like many other things, this very often took place in the evenings, at the College Tree. This tree, which is still standing opposite the Muckross Hotel, was a kind of unofficial, outdoor version of the clubhouse. As Danny Cronin put it: *''Twas there the college was at night. There was a lot of fellows educated there!'*

It was at the College Tree, for example, that the Biddies used to meet, before setting off on their rounds. The Biddies were one of the high points of the year's social round in Muckross, and Dr Kevin Danaher makes mention of the Muckross Biddies in his book *The Year in Ireland* (Cork 1972). On the night before 1 February, St Bridget's Day, groups of young people would disguise themselves and would go from house to house in the area. With them they would carry the Biddy, which was a kind of crudely-fashioned doll, often made from rags and boards and a turnip. They would sing and dance in each house, usually to the music of an accordion, and they would ask for *'something for the Biddy'*. In most cases, they got money. The night would end with a dance in somebody's house, although in later years the dance was held in the Lake Hotel.

From the accounts I got of social life in Muckross, it seems clear that workers and tenants – big and small – socialised together, and that the 'gentry' socialised separately. Whenever the twain did meet – as, for example, when the landlord gave a dance for the servants in the coachhouse – social roles were still rigidly adhered to, and there was no real closing of the gap. It would apparently have taken more than a dance to shake people out of their prescribed roles and modes of behaviour.

Conclusion

Today, the wheel has come full circle, and many of the sons and daughters of former estate workers are now employed in the national park. Tenants of the Big House might come and go, but the people of Muckross have remained, and have preserved customs and traditions many of which have been handed down from generation to generation with their origins in a time long before that of Muckross House.

My sincere thanks are due to Kevin Danaher, Danny and Josie Cronin, Billy Vincent, Michael and Mary O'Connor, Paudie and Sheila Cremin, Brian O'Shea, Rita Doody, all those mentioned in this chapter and everyone else who helped with my work in Muckross. A final word of appreciation must go to the late Ned Myers, former manager of Muckross House.

*My research in Muckross was carried out as part of my work in the Department of Irish Folklore. The principal source materials for the present chapter were the tape-recorded interviews which I made in the Muckross area in the early 1980s, as described above. I have also made use of the Manuscript Collections in the Department of Irish Folklore, University College Dublin, with the kind permission of the Head of the Department, Professor Séamas Ó Catháin. I also consulted the unpublished work by Jacinta McCullagh, 'Land Ownership in the Parish of Killarney, 1800–1907', (*c.*1978), a copy of which is in Muckross House. I am also very grateful to Séan Ryan, author of chapter 9 in this volume, for his advice on a number of points.

Chapter 8

Lakes and Rivers

Bill Quirke

If the landscape of Killarney speaks it is with a voice of water. Water gurgling along invisible channels beneath the mountain peat, chattering along mountain streams, curling and plunging in floods over cascades and waterfalls, lapping the shores of the park's many lakes, or breaking in white-capped storm waves. Water, maybe the purest and least contaminated in Europe, is transported in generous quantity from the nearby Atlantic by an endless procession of weather systems from the southwest.

Occasionally, high pressure continental weather prevails for a few weeks, but a couple of weeks without rain in Killarney is an unusual event. The mosses look tired, the ferns growing along the branches of the trees and on old walls begin to droop and wilt, the mountains become vague and insubstantial with haze. If you are in Killarney when the weather finally breaks at the end of a settled sunny spell, put on your rain coat and wellingtons and get out into the woods and mountains. There you will experience a landscape coming alive. All around streams have awakened and the steep mountainsides are streaked by ribbons of white. Make your way south from Killarney town along the road to Kenmare and you can visit Torc waterfall at its most dramatic. Torc, although the only one signposted, is just one of many beautiful waterfalls and cascades in the national park. Carry on south where the road rounds the flank of Torc mountain; here you enter a landscape of wild mountains and woodlands. To your right the Long Range, an untamed and unpolluted river, is rising fast with the surge of water unleashed through the Black Valley and the Upper Lake from the high Macgillycuddys Reeks. The river can rise by over one metre in 24 hours of heavy rain, inundating the flood plain on either side. In August 1986 the water rose high enough to wash away parts of the wall bordering the road at the 'Five Mile Bridge', more than three metres above the dry weather level. From here,

Derrycunihy cascade after heavy rain. (Padraig O'Donoghue)

After heavy rain the mountainsides are streaked with ribbons of white. (Padraig O'Donoghue)

across the river and beyond the Eagle's Nest crag, looms the remote Glaisín na Marbh valley. *Glaisín na Marbh* means 'little stream of the dead', and tradition holds that in famine times a burial ground existed in the valley. The burial ground is lost, but the Glaisín in flood still stands out white through the ancient woodland. Now ahead of you the precipitous face of Cromaglan Mountain, clothed in wild woodland, is threaded through by a plunging stream of white, falling 200 metres from tiny Lough Crincaun hidden above. The road pierces the flank of the mountain through 'the tunnel'. From this

Long Range River and Eagle's Nest Mountain. (Bill Quirke)

The Upper Lake.
(Bill Quirke)

road you can see the essences of Killarney; wild forests and mountains unspoiled by human interference, and beneath you the Upper of the three main lakes of the national park.

The Lakes of Killarney – how can one evoke them? For two centuries and longer the object of superlative and hyperbole, now almost a cliché of beauty. 'By Killarney's lakes and fells', 'Heaven's reflex Killarney', 'How can you buy Killarney?' 'Beauty's home'; old slogans to bolster the confidence of a burgeoning and ambitious tourist industry. But today's visitor may well come away wondering what all the fuss was about. The beauty of Killarney, like its wildlife, reveals itself to those who take their time. Attempt to rush it and you may find a disappointing greyness, or at best a glimpse of extraordinary beauty that you cannot grasp, that you don't have the time to discover and must delegate to your camera in the hope that some day you may have the time to really appreciate the significance of what you have seen. With time you may see winter days on Lough Leane when the pastel pink and purple of the leafless alders and willows are softened by a frosty mist, or when cormorants, flying a mile away across the water, sound clearly and

Lough Leane: O'Donoghue's Prison and Inisfallen. (Bill Quirke)

form perfect symmetries with their reflected wings. You may see islands raising their tree shapes above a lake of mist or, after floods, wallowing knee-deep like half sunk boats. You may see lakes washed with sunset and paved by moonlight. You may see the water churning with white-topped waves, spray whipped up into ominous spirals by a curling storm.

Indeed Killarney's lakes are as beautiful as anyone has ever written, but to find them takes the unhurried time that many visitors seem to lack. Until 1978 visitors were rowed through the lakes in traditional 'gap boats' with four oarsmen. Until 1992 one boatman carried on the centuries old tradition of rowing visitors on the lakes in the same way his father did and many generations before. Now most of the traditional boats are motor driven. The first waterbus which was launched on Lough Leane in 1986 was soon joined by a second significantly larger craft. The original has since been replaced by a craft more than twice its size.

Water is the life of the landscape. Every tiny area of mountain and wood in the park has its tiny stream capillaries which supply the great river arteries

The first water bus on Lough Leane. (Bill Quirke)

which pulse to the rhythm of the weather and the seasons, feeding the lakes which ceaselessly swell and subside, the Upper Lake almost visibly rising and falling, the Middle and Lower lakes following at a more relaxed pace.

As well as giving life to the landscape the rivers and lakes of the park are home to an astonishing community of living creatures, invisible and unexpected to the uninitiated. As is the case in the woods and mountains, an intricate web of life thrives in the world of water. This web of life is sustained by a constant supply of nutrients dissolved in the water and in the form of soil, peat and plant debris washed into the rivers. The greater the supply of nutrients, the more abundant the growth of plant life in the water, both visible and microscopic. The more plentiful the plant growth, the

more abundant are the animals which feed on them; a menagerie of strange and wonderful animals, mostly tiny clinging, crawling and burrowing animals. These tiny animals in turn provide food for hunting animals, ranging in size from tiny water beetles to fish, herons and otters. The amount of nutrients available has a dominant influence on life in this water world. In the high mountain streams the soil is thin and acid, and the old red sandstone releases only miserly supplies of nutrients to the eroding rain. So life here is fairly sparse, but what is there is perfectly adapted to eking out a living in the mountain torrents.

Many of these animals, such as the juvenile stoneflies, are flat and streamlined, with strong clinging legs and claws to allow them to stay put despite the fact that their river universe is in constant motion, always downstream. These are the experts at holding on, sucking on, clinging on, finding the shelter of rocks and eddies – the daredevils of the mountain torrents. Further downstream, the rivers become better supplied with nutrients. Some flow through the limestone areas of the park; here the soil is richer and the rivers support more plant growth and a corresponding abundance of animals. What seems to the uninformed eye to be just a weedy river is a jungle of living creatures, hunting and hiding, ambushing and grazing; animals such as the larva

129

The Upper Lake.
(Seán Ryan)

of the caddis fly which armours itself in a transportable tube of pebbles, sand or pieces of plants; animals with snorkels, animals with spears, animals with nets. Here the young trout, hatched further upstream, spend their early lives in the nursery stream before descending to the lakes. Here the salmon start the long journey down to the lakes and down the River Laune to the ocean. The vast majority of brown trout migrate to the lake from the spawning streams as one year-old fish. Most mature in their second year, but only a small proportion of trout spawn in any one year. Their life expectancy is relatively short, with few brown trout living to more than three years of age.

The lakes are home to even more mysterious communities of plants and animals. Here, as in the rivers, the supply of nutrients is a vital factor. All the small mountain lakes and the Upper and Middle Lakes have low nutrient levels, because all their water flows from the acid sandstone mountains. Low nutrients mean sparse growth of plants and few of the tiny microscopic plants that float as plankton in the surface waters. Because the plankton is so sparse, the water is clear and in the Middle Lake you can peer six or seven metres into the depths. Sparse plant growth also means meagre rations for the animals. If you pass by boat from the Middle Lake under Brickeen Bridge into the Lower Lake you will notice a sudden reduction in water clarity and a dramatic change in the animal life. More boats with anglers, cormorants lined up on rocks, herons stalking the shallows, all indicate more fish and bigger fish. Here, if you rummage under the stones in the shallows, you will find tiny animals in amazing abundance – tens of thousands in a square metre. All of this indicates a lake that is rich in nutrients. Even 60 metres down in the dark profundal zone of the lake, the sediments are alive with insect larvae and worms, sustained by the rain of tiny plants and animals, manna from the sunlit surface far above.

The variety of life in the lakes is far greater than might be expected. Many insects spend only their brief maturity in the air; most of their lives are spent on the bottom of the lakes. Most people are surprised to hear that there are both biting and non-biting types of midges. The news that the larvae of more than 150 different types of non-biting midges are to be found living in the Killarney lakes and rivers is a surprise indeed. Though often hardly bigger than an eyelash, these tiny creatures often have impressive names. A species of midge inhabits the Lower Lake, no doubt oblivious of its glorious name – *Paralauterborniella nigrohalteralis*.

Better known are the fish of the lakes. A major study of the fish of the Killarney Lakes completed in 1990, listed nineteen fish species/varieties in the Killarney Lakes catchment: sea lamprey, river lamprey, brook lamprey, allis shad, Killarney twaite shad, salmon, sea trout, brown trout, ferox trout, char, tench, gudgeon, minnow, stone loach, eel, three-spined stickleback, ten-spined stickleback, perch, and flounder. Roach were found in Lough Leane for the first time in 1991.

Several species of fish found in the Killarney lakes are of particular interest. The Killarney shad, a little herring-like fish, is a unique landlocked variety of the twaite shad. Other populations exclusive to freshwater occur in some Italian lakes. The char, normally a fish of the sub-Arctic, is presumably a relict species. More widely spread in glacial and post glacial times, as the climate became milder, its range contracted to a small number of Irish water bodies, including Lough Leane. Flounder, locally known as fluke, make their way up the river Laune from the ocean to Lough Leane. The ferox trout or 'great lake trout' is considered to be a distinct form of brown trout, possibly the descendants of an ancestral trout lineage which entered Ireland after the Ice Age. Ferox trout show a marked increase in growth rate between the fourth and eighth years of life. This spurt in growth rate is attributed to the trout changing to a predominantly fish diet. While considered to be rare by anglers, in the 1990 study they constituted 3.6 per cent of the total number of trout caught.

Fishing, particularly for salmon, has probably been an important activity on the Killarney lakes since the stone age hunter gatherers first came to the area. Isaac Weld's account published in 1807 shows that at that time salmon fishing was a significant aspect of the local economy and a valued part of the tourist diet.

> The bay of Glena is remarkable for the best salmon fishery on the lake. This and the other fisheries are leased out, at a small annual rent, under a condition that no more than two-pence a pound shall be demanded for the produce in the town of Killarney. All persons, however, are freely allowed to angle in the lake and in its rivers. The nets are commonly cast along a spacious inlet, just under Glena mountain, where occasionally very large draughts of fish are taken; and in the season they are seldom drawn without taking some. At all entertainments on the lake, salmon forms an essential part of the feast. The men, for a small gratuity, will postpone drawing their nets till the time of dinner approaches; and an hour after the fish swims in the lake it is served at table. The mode of dressing it, in which the men display much expertness, is to cut it in pieces, which are roasted on fresh cut twigs of the arbutus tree stuck in the ground before a smart fire made of dried leaves and sticks.

The lakes, particularly the shallower shores and bays of Lough Leane, are still popular for salmon and trout angling, with most anglers fishing from their own boats. The Central Fisheries Board carried out a fish survey in 1991 and Lough Leane was found to be one of Ireland's premier salmonid lake fisheries. The survey indicated a very large trout population in the range of 671,840 trout greater than 19.8 cm in length. The survey states that:

> the current angling effort for this species is not in any significant way affecting the stock. Indeed data indicate that a very considerably increased

angler cropping rate could be sustained without unduly affecting stocks. Consequently, a significant increase in tourist angling effort could be accommodated. This is of particular value to the local community because the best trout angling months (April, May, June and September) are shoulder periods in the general tourist season.

The fish share the lakes' bounty with, and sometimes themselves serve as food for, the otters and mink and the diverse birdlife. There have been 34 species of water bird recorded on the Lakes of Killarney. Species which breed on the lakes include: little grebe, great-crested grebe, grey heron, mute swan, teal, mallard, tufted duck, red-breasted merganser, coot, moorhen and water rail. Some species such as the cormorant are present around the year but not breeding in the park. In winter the lakes are enlivened by teal, pochard, gold-eneye, wigeon, Bewick's swan and whooper swans, migrating into the park from areas such as Iceland and Northern Europe. Other species are rare or vagrant such as the red-throated diver and the spotted crake which were recorded only once, and occasionally recorded species such as the great northern diver, shelduck, gadwall, pintail, garganey, shoveller, ring-necked

Mute swans. (Paudie O'Leary)

Castlelough Bay on Lough Leane. (Paudie O'Leary)

duck, long-tailed duck, common scoter and goosander. Eight wader species (two recorded as breeding) have been recorded on the lake margins. Heron, kingfisher and dipper are regularly seen on flowing waters and all breed in the park. Hatching aquatic insects also provide food for the swallows, martins and swifts which feed over the lakes. Very occasionally a solitary migrating osprey visits the lakes, a reminder of the ospreys that inhabited the lakes area until the last century. Thus a total of over 50 bird species frequent lakes and rivers and their margins.

Large assemblages of water birds can be a striking sight at certain times of year. The largest species of waterfowl on Lough Leane are the mute swans, of which an average of six to ten pairs breed on the lake; however, by late June, the population of nesting swans is augmented to as many as 90 by an influx of non-breeders or failed breeders. Large numbers (up to 570) of mallard are attracted during good acorn years to the Killarney lakes, where they will forage along the shoreline beneath the oaks. The breeding population of coot is augmented in autumn, with 'rafts' of 60 or more birds being quite common in the past. As many as 100 cormorants live on the Lower Lake; they can be seen lining the limestone reefs close to the Muckross shore, diving for fish or flying low across the water. Although sometimes regarded as competitors by anglers, cormorants may prey more on eels and other coarse fish, and so may benefit the trout stocks.

Defining where the lake ends and the land begins is an impossible task along the lowland shores of Lough Leane, and we could justifiably describe woodlands and red deer as components of the lake's flora and fauna. During wetter weather the lake spreads into the wet swampy woodlands which border much of the lake (see Chapter 10). In several areas as you approach the shore from open water, pure reed beds become reed beds with alder trees, which in turn become reedy alder woods, which in turn become dense swamp woodlands, which eventually merge with dryer woodland, grassland or bog. This transition from open water to dryland vegetation reflects in space a transition which also takes place in the shallow waters of the lake over time. Areas of shallow open water gradually become shallower as sediment is deposited and dead bottom-growing plants accumulate. Eventually the water becomes shallow enough for reeds to grow. The process of accumulating dead plant material and sediments continues until the water becomes shallow enough for swamp woodland trees such as alder to colonise. Eventually the woodland may take over entirely.

One of the most interesting park wildlife discoveries in recent years has been revealed by an ongoing study of the lowland red deer. For many years it had been noted that the numbers of red deer seen in the lowland area of the park close to Killarney town declined dramatically during the summer months. Even night counts using spotlights revealed few red deer at this time of year and it was presumed that the deer left the area and migrated to the less disturbed mountain areas. The present study indicates that though the deer disappear, most of them remain in the area. This is achieved by the deer becoming in a sense 'semi-aquatic'. The one place where they are guaranteed total seclusion from people and dogs, particularly during the calving period, is in the extensive lake reed beds, on the little dryer clumps of alder 'islands' in the reed beds and in the dense swamp woodlands that fringe the eastern shores of Lough Leane. Out in the reed beds they may also get welcome respite from biting insects which plague them on calm summer days. This

Brickeen Bridge where Muckross lake flows into Lough Leane. (Paudie O'Leary)

swampy refuge area provides ample forage with little need to use the more exposed areas of open pasture. With the return of higher water levels in winter the deer move out of the lake reedbeds and swamp woodland into the dryer woods and open pastures where they are more easily seen. By this means a truly wild population of red deer, which now numbers close to 100 animals, has managed to survive and prosper in an area that is within a stag's roar of Killarney town, one of the busiest tourist centres in the country.

Over the centuries the diverse flora and fauna of the Killarney lakes visible to the eye of scientists and visiting naturalists have cohabited with the legendary and mythological inhabitants of the lake. As far back as 1756 Charles Smith in his *'Ancient and present state of the County of Kerry'* wrote that:

> the common people hereabouts, have a strange romantic notion, of their seeing in fair weather, what they call a carbuncle, at the bottom of this lake, in a particular part of it, which they say is more than 60 fathoms deep.

Reen Point and reed bed.
(Bill Quirke)

Smith was not the first person to mistakenly assume that the boatmen were referring to a precious stone. The true nature of the carbuncle was learned by a botanist called Henry Hart when exploring the Kerry mountains in 1883. He learned that it was also to be seen in a lake on the Dingle peninsula where the people, who collected freshwater mussels for the pearls, informed him that the mussels: 'Come off an enormous animal called the carrabuncle, which is often seen glittering like silver in the water at night'. Five years later another naturalist named Nathaniel Colgan further investigated the legend. The local people confirmed the fact of the carrabuncle's existence but added that it was seen only once in seven years, and then it lights up the whole lake. A strange tale, but stranger still because the famous scientist Alfred Russel Wallace heard accounts of a similar mythical water-monster called the 'Carabunculo' on his explorations of the Upper Amazon and Peru in the 1840s. In 1937 Ireland's most esteemed naturalist Robert Lloyd Praeger suggested that the probable explanation of the presence of the name in these two widely-separated areas lies in the fact that both regions were in intimate connection with Spain.

*Doo Lough on the
Muckross Peninsula.
(Bill Quirke)*

The Killarney conservationist, Michael O'Sullivan, has suggested an intriguing interpretation of the carrabuncle legend. The sturgeon (*Acipenser sturio*), a fish which regularly reaches lengths of 6 ft (2 m) and can reach over 11 ft (3.4 m) in length is a vagrant visitor to the freshwaters of these islands. Endangered now throughout its range, it was more widespread and abundant in the past. Sturgeons, though mainly marine, spawn in freshwaters in large rivers and sometimes lakes. The hard bony protruding plates (carbuncles?) along the backs and sides of the sturgeon are not dissimilar in appearance to freshwater pearl mussels protruding from a river bottom, and it is easy to see how the connection might have been made by the people of Kerry in past centuries if sturgeons actually entered Kerry rivers and lakes. Given that modern accounts describe the sturgeon as a 'magnificent fish' with a 'shiny plated body', the nineteenth-century description of 'an enormous animal . . . glittering like silver', could conceivably be accurate.

Whether great sturgeons occasionally made their way up the river Laune and into the lakes of Killarney giving rise to the legend of the wondrous carrabuncle we can only guess; however, the freshwater pearl mussels once thought to have been spawned by the carrabuncle still survive in some of the rivers flowing into the lakes of Killarney National Park. The freshwater pearl mussel *Margaritifera margaritifera* is becoming increasingly rare in Ireland and is threatened with extinction throughout the world, due to pollution, habitat destruction and exploitation. These shellfish can grow up to 150 mm long and may live for up to 150 years. Pearl mussels have occupied a special place in the fauna of the Killarney area for over 1,000 years. In the year 900 a monk Nennius wrote of Lough Leane, 'in the lake many pearls are found that kings place in their ears'. Sir Richard Cox wrote in 1687 that 'Pearls, Large, Orient and in great Quantities are got out ye Lough (Lough Leane)'. In a strange echo of the old folklore, the pearl mussel does indeed depend for its survival on being carried by a fish. The early larval stage of the mollusc is spent on the gills of trout or salmon, whereby the sedentary mussel can renew its population upstream in fast flowing rivers.

All of the lake life, from the microscopic animals up to the duck, fish and otters, is ultimately dependent on the nutrients taken from the water

Algal bloom in Lough Leane 1983. (Bill Quirke)

139

and the energy taken from sunlight by the plant life of the lakes. Under totally natural conditions Lough Leane would have a moderate supply of nutrients because some of its water flows out of nutrient-rich limestone areas. In recent times this natural supply of nutrients was greatly augmented by nutrients contained in wastewater entering the lake from Killarney town and surrounding areas. A lot of nutrients have also entered the lake from agricultural activities in the catchment of the River Flesk, which is outside the national park but flows into the Lower Lake. Over the years the town has grown, and more and more homes and hotels have connected their waste water to the town sewage system. Until 1985 the waste water from the town received inadequate treatment before being released into the Lower Lake at Ross Bay. Ecological monitoring of the lakes was started in 1971 and continued virtually unbroken until the present day. This 'diary of a lake' provides a fascinating record of the effects of artificial nutrient enrichment of the lake, culminating in 1983 in a major 'bloom' of blue-green algae, with dramatic effects on all the life forms of the lake.

In 1983 the conditions in the Lower Lake were ideally suited to the growth of tiny floating plants called blue-green algae. It was a calm, sunny, warm summer, and a plentiful supply of nutrients was provided by the Killarney town sewer. In mid July, strange silvery flecks appeared in the water throughout the lake. Within a few weeks much of the lake had the appearance of pea soup or green emulsion paint, as the countless billions of tiny blue-green algae proliferated in the surface waters. Such a bloom can often result in the fish suffocating, because all the oxygen dissolved in the water can be used up as the algae rot. Luckily this did not happen in Lough Leane because of the depth of the lake. A similar, though less visible, bloom occurred in 1984. The effects of the blooms were detected throughout the web of life in the lake. Sixty metres down in the dark profundal sediments, aquatic worms increased in numbers because of the increased 'rain' of food from above, while insect larvae declined. In shallower waters, rooted plants and algae growing on the bottom died away because little light could penetrate the 'pea soup' of algae in the water. Many tiny creatures which inhabit the lake shallows are sensitive to lake enrichment and declined dramatically. For the animals that could cope, the increased supply of plant food resulted in rich feeding, and though anglers rightly fear the effects of algal blooms,

Glena Bay in Lough Leane during 1983 algal bloom. (Bill Quirke)

the effect of the enrichment of Lough Leane over the years was to increase the food supply and thus increase the average size of fish.

In 1985 a major improvement of the sewage treatment facilities was completed which could remove much of the nutrients from the waste water. For the next five to seven years the growth of algae declined and unsightly deposits of decomposing algae on the shores became less of a problem. To keep pace with the expanding tourist industry a major upgrading of Killarney's sewerage system and a further expansion of the sewage treatment facilities was carried out. Nevertheless, in the 1990s the sum of nutrient inputs to Lough Leane from the entire catchment increased again, culminating in 1997 in an algal bloom of even greater severity than the bloom of 1983. The 1997 bloom resulted in the total deoxygenation of the deepest waters of the lake. Without oxygen most of the invertebrate animals of the deepest lake bottom sediments died off. Again, as in 1983, a major fish kill was avoided, though results of a fish survey carried out by the Central Fisheries Board in 1999 showed reduced trout and shad stocks as compared with their 1991 survey. A major challenge is now being faced: to identify the most important nutrient inputs in the catchment and reduce them. To this end a large scale project – the Lough Leane Catchment Monitoring and Management System – is now being implemented by Kerry County Council, with government funding in excess of £1 million.

With vigilance and care Lough Leane can again reflect the mountains and sky in its clear water. Thankfully, the Upper Lake, Muckross Lake and Looscaunagh Lake as well as the numerous smaller mountain lakes and streams of the national park, remain largely pure and uncontaminated; a rare and precious heritage in an increasingly polluted world.

Chapter 9

The Mountains

Seán Ryan

Introduction

The scenery of Killarney National Park is dominated by mountains. Whereas the park's woods and lakes are somewhat distinct and self contained, the park's mountain boundaries are highly artificial. For example, Mangerton Mountain, and likewise Purple Mountain, are both cut in half by straight line boundaries. Outside the park boundaries and flanking it to the south-east lies the magnificent mountain complex of Lough Guitane. Just outside the park to the west are the significantly higher Reeks, which provide a spectacular mountain landscape of heavily glaciated high coums, back-to-back and separated by frost-shattered narrow arêtes or rock ridges, as well as classic hanging valleys and moraine structures. This is the highest land in Ireland, and has been called a masterpiece of the Ice Age. Although outside the park, these mountains form the backdrop, the borrowed scenery on which the park so heavily relies for much of its spectacular landscapes, and consequently are also dealt with in this chapter.

In the park itself mountain land over 300 metres in altitude comprises about one-third of the land area; high mountain, 600 metres and above, comprises less than 5 per cent of the park's land. The park's mountains fall naturally into two groups, divided by the Killarney Valley and Lake system. South of the Valley lies the Mangerton/Torc range (max. altitude 837 metres), which includes the lower hills of Knockrower, Stompacoumeen and Cromaglan. This is an area of relatively gentle slopes, with several small mountain lakes, and many swiftly tumbling mountain streams. Mangerton's summit is a broad expansive plateau, with heavily eroded peat hags; its north cliffs fall into

The view from Torc Mountain across the Long Range River to the western mountains of the park and the peaks of Purple Mountain and the Reeks. (Seán Ryan)

Mountains such as the Reeks, seen here from the Upper Lake, form the backdrop, the borrowed scenery on which the Park so heavily relies for much of its spectacular landscapes. (Seán Ryan)

the magnificent ice-gouged coum of Gleann na gCapall, which itself lies outside the park. North of the valley lies the Purple/Tomies/Shehy/Glena group (max. altitude 832 metres) with its steeper slopes, more pointed summits, and extensive scree on Purple Mountain. Its character is more akin to the adjacent higher Reeks, from which it is separated by the great north-south gash of the Gap of Dunloe.

The Mountain Climate

Like all mountain land these areas experience climatic extremes. Mangerton's summit plateau and Purple's pointed cone are both prone to some snow cover every winter; on lower slopes below 600 metres, snow lies for a much shorter period. It was not always so. Writing in 1687 a visitor to Killarney remarked that the summit of Mangerton was rarely without snow even in mid-summer. This is likely to have been a true record, as Europe experienced a mini-ice age from the mid-sixteenth to the mid-nineteenth centuries, during which snowlie on Mangerton into late June would have been quite possible. Even in the milder climate of today, snow can lie on the highest ridges and summits of the Reeks from late October to mid-May during a long and severe winter which occasionally occurs.

However, the more usual mountain winters of Killarney National Park are likely to be characterised by extensive periods of rain, and strong winds, with an occasional spell of prolonged frost. It is not only the quantity of rain (up to 4,000 mm per annum have been recorded), but its prolonged duration which has such an impact on these mountains; some precipitation occurs on 300 days, or more, of every year. Such extended periods of rain, together with frequent high winds, the cooler temperatures of high altitude, and extensive cloud cover obscuring direct sunlight for much of the year, combine to give a pattern of long, cold, wet and windy winters, and short, cool, damp and windy summers. The persistent rainfall also leaches from the mountain soils much of the already limited nutrients which the underlying acidic rocks release by a very slow weathering. It is a harsh and demanding environment, influencing all life on the mountains, and ultimately dictating what type of organisms will survive there. Relatively few species of plants and animals are adapted to live in these exacting conditions. But the species that can tolerate them (such as some insect species) may have vast populations and are often grouped into fascinating communities of plants and animals specially adapted to the rigours of life at high altitudes.

Mountain Experiences

The mountains of Killarney National Park are but a small part of the mountain complexes of the Greater Killarney Area. All are rugged and gloriously wild. One of the most important aspects of this heritage is the experience of wildness; accepting the mountain and its wildlife for its own intrinsic beauty. What follows is an account of some of the experiences which these mountains have to offer, through the seasons.

SUMMER

Summers are brief and come late. It is early June before the fresh growth of new grasses reaches the highest summits. *Molinia*, or purple moor grass, is a predominant plant; the fresh vivid greens of its young growth are a delight

In early June the fresh growth of new grasses reaches the highest summits. Into this brief period of plenty the young red deer calves are born. (Paudie O'Leary)

to the eye and a source of attraction to the red deer which now avidly graze it. It forms extensive tussocks, especially in wet seepage hollows. Also growing now are the sedges which flower in late June and early July; a level expanse of high bog, covered with the fluffy white seed heads of cotton sedge, dancing and tossing in a summer breeze against a background of purple-blue hills, is a most memorable sight and well worth the effort of going up to see, year after year. The season's green growth is evident everywhere, and into this brief period of plenty the young red deer calves are born. The calf lies concealed and quite still for two to three days, its white-spotted red/brown back a bit incongruous in the new greens of summer. By its second or third day it can outrun a man. Soon the mother and calf units will coalesce into nursery bands, and then one of the great wildlife sights of the park hills occurs, as the red deer aggregate into large herds, sometimes numbering up to 150 animals. This happens from late July into early August.

Occasionally a succession of high-pressure weather systems brings a hot and dry spell; then the distant hills shimmer and swim in the heat, all detail is lost, and only their outlines stand out through a blue heat haze. Such days are likely to be plagued by countless myriads of biting midges and flies; to escape these, deer travel far uphill, seeking relief in the winds of the summit. Mostly, however, the summer is wet and windy, ideal conditions for bog plants to flourish, such as the diminutive sundews, small insectivorous plants on the wetter bogs which well repay close examination. Bog myrtle, a common dwarf shrub of the lower wet slopes, is also worth investigating; its leaves when crushed in the hand produce a hauntingly beautiful and lingering aroma.

Mountain streams are at low volume, affording an opportunity to pause and admire the beauty and colours of their water polished stone beds. Sometimes the high streams shrink to a succession of shallow pools in which an occasional small brown trout darts in swift zigzags. This must be one of the reasons why herons come upland to stalk the high streams. On the larger mountain lakes, for example in Gleann na gCapall, cormorants also come to dive and fish. Common birds of the mountain stream side are the grey wagtail, which is never still, and the dipper. To observe a dipper searching the merest trickle of a high stream and the tiniest of pools, overgrown by dense grass tussocks, is a lesson in survival. Lucky indeed is the person who chances to glimpse the elusive and rare ring ouzel. When the sun comes out between the showers, you can watch dragon-flies and damsel-flies hover above the black waters of shallow bog pools. Their larvae are buried in the water-saturated peat of the pool edges. On rare still days many insects can be seen up high; red admiral and peacock butterflies in small groups at about 600 metres on the slopes of Mangerton; even on its summit plateau some ground beetles that have made the long journey up here.

The highest summits offer perhaps the most rewarding of true wilderness experiences. Lichens, the first colonisers of rock and scree, form colourful patchwork patterns. All plant life is dwarfed; low-growing and spreading, or compact and cushion-shaped, hugging the soil to take advantage of the micro-climate at ground level. At this elevation a few inches can make all the difference in terms of shelter and temperature. Bilberry is here reduced to an inch or two, but it is mostly the mosses, especially woolly hairmoss which form the attractive and spongy carpets of the summit ridges, good examples being the slopes of Purple or the ridge of Mangerton North. The cushion plants are compact, hard, dense and rounded, ensuring that the maximum of foliage is presented to catch any available sunlight and warmth. A beautiful example is sea thrift growing at 900 and 1,000 metres on the Reeks, where it forms tight, dense mounds, flowering later than at sea level. These compact mounds can withstand long snowlie and extensive exposure; they are usually browned and wind-burned on the weather side, they themselves providing a micro-habitat for tiny organisms which huddle in the shelter of their lee. Unfortunately they are often trampled and kicked to pieces by the passage of many climbers' boots, something which could easily be avoided

Roseroot, a rare plant of the high mountain cliffs, grows among the dark crags of the Reeks. (Seán Ryan)

by a little care and feeling for the beauty of their pink flowers. High mountain ecology is particularly fragile, and damage to such slow-growing plant communities takes years to heal. Some of the rare and exquisitely beautiful plants cling to the steep north faces of these high mountains, places accessible to disciplined and experienced climbers. The sight of a community of roseroot on the black cliffs of the north face of Caher in the Reeks, flooded by sunlight streaming down over the Caher ridge, can provide climbers with a shock of sheer visual impact that is unsurpassed in mountain wildness. While enjoying the Reeks, it is well worth traversing the skyline of the Beanncaorach-Carrauntoohil arête to inspect a superb example of fossilised shallow sea or lake floor, uplifted here to 900 metres.

If it has been a dry summer, there comes with August the delicate and delicious scent of rain. The moist atmosphere heightens colour; the yellow flower spikes of bog asphodel gleam and glow amongst the grasses and sedges. A typical weather pattern is wet or showery forenoon with afternoon and evening sunshine. In late summer it is sometimes rewarding to keep absolutely still by the old rubble stone walls on the lower hills of the park;

149

then a lizard comes out to bask in the late evening sunshine, and quietly dozes off asleep.

Down in the lowlands, the summer tourist numbers are about to peak, but here in the mountains, the first signs of autumn are already evident.

AUTUMN

Autumn comes early, and is brief. By mid-August daylight is noticeably shorter and the evenings on the hillsides are noticeably cold. Already the deer sedge at 300 metres is beginning to colour, its tips turning a yellow brown. It is the flowering time of the heathers of which three types are found in the park hills; the common ling and bell heathers on drier more rocky slopes, and the cross-leaved heath in the wetter areas. All have the well-known purple flowers. The extensive stand of heather on Shehy and Purple Mountain was burned out in the great mountain fire of 1984 which swept across the Eagle's Nest, up Glaisín na Marbh, over the broad rounded back of Shehy and into Coumcloughane, until it finally burned itself out on the high scree slopes of Purple Mountain.

On much of the drier slopes, heather is mixed with the yellow blooms of the dwarf furze, sometimes forming a tight colourful mat of purple and gold. This is the dwarf furze which we once called *aiteann Gaelach* (Irish furze), to distinguish it from the introduced and taller *aiteann Gallda* (foreign furze). The dwarf furze grows to 600 metres and above. An extensive tract, blazing a golden yellow in October, was one of the glories of Cloughfune on the southwest of Torc; it has been burned out in a mountain fire. At high altitude the dwarf furze becomes tighter, growing in compact mounds, mixed with stunted heather and bilberry. On the lower slopes it is taller, providing both shelter and winter greens for deer.

This is the time when nature is preparing for next year's regeneration. Bright red berries glow on mountain ash and occasional whitethorn. In a year of great abundance, isolated mountain ash trees which survive by stream beds are a fuzz of scarlet berries. Woodpigeon flock to the feast, and the droppings of mountain foxes are mostly of berry seeds as they gorge on the plentiful supply before winter. The insects also prepare. The dark brown hairy caterpillar that is commonly seen on grass and sedge is that of the fox-moth. Being conspicuous is not a problem, since its survival is ensured by its

Few wilderness experiences in all of Irish wildlife can equal the thrill of lying on the heather on a high mountain slope, listening to the roaring of the red deer stags. (Seán Ryan)

sticky and irritating hairs which adhere to the inside of a predator's mouth, and foxes have learned to leave it alone. The opposite occurs in the case of the caterpillar of the emperor moth; its survival strategy is perfect camouflage. A strikingly beautiful insect of bright green with bands of purple, it perfectly resembles the flowering shoots of ling heather on which it feeds.

The deer also prepare. October is the time of the rut, or mating season, for the red deer. A population of Japanese sika deer, introduced in the last century, also inhabits the hills and woods of the national park. The sika rut, though beginning in late August, also lasts throughout the mountain autumn. It is perhaps the most exciting, and certainly the most spectacular time to observe the deer on the national park hills. Few wilderness experiences in all of Irish wildlife can equal the thrill of lying on the heather on a high mountain slope, listening to the roaring of the red deer stags. If you are lucky enough to enjoy the rare luxury of a dry hillside, and have succeeded in stalking close, the resonance of a red stag's deep, guttural roar will seem to penetrate your being. Not too close; no stag can be trusted during the rut. Roaring usually peaks in late evening before dusk; then the hills and high

The view from Cores Mountain looking west. (Seán Ryan)

coums resound and echo to the roaring of many stags. Such continuous bouts of roaring can last for up to twenty minutes, with a roar occurring from different stags about every two seconds. The sika's rutting call is altogether different; a loud shrill and piercing whistle-scream, repeated three times, or occasionally just once. Fights between competing males occur every year, but are seldom witnessed. To witness a stag fight between two large red stags is to experience the ultimate in wildness. But keep your distance; these stags are utterly wild, large and powerful, and incredibly swift.

As autumn progresses, the first thin films of ice appear on bog pools, and the grasses and sedges wither into the magnificent russets, golden-yellows and luminous red browns which are the glory of the Kerry hills, especially when sunlit at evening. Amid the short cropped heathers of the drier mounds, the withering leaves of bilberry flash a brilliant scarlet. Into this colourful world of upland bog come the winter bird visitors; a flock of greenland white-fronted geese fly in about mid-October (see Chapter 11). Watching them and listening to their calls as they fly over the hills into a frosty dusk is a memorable experience. As the cold increases, small flocks of golden plover, now in winter plumage, settle into the tundra-like red-brown vegetation of the higher slopes; their piping plaintive calls form one of the most evocative sounds of the late autumn hills. They do not stay, however, and quickly pass on, leaving the hills to the sighing of the winds. But the autumn hills are not as empty as they may casually appear. A careful observer can sometimes see a short-eared owl, or a female hen harrier, a large raptor with a conspicuous white rump which frequents the lower hills, quartering and beating up and across the slopes.

Autumn is often a time of frequent storms and high winds, when the hills are blotted out in grey sheets of driving rain. This too has its own wondrous beauty. In the darkly clouded and moisture saturated atmosphere, the lichens seem to glow underfoot with a silver luminescence. Up in the high coums the storm's fury can be fully experienced. Banks of grey-white cloud pour over the coum's upper rim and cascade down across the black cliff-face until the whole coum is a seething mass of boiling cloud, yet even in the shrieking wind and into the teeth of the gale, a black raven flies. Such wind and rain storms can be exacting and punishing, but weather, too, is part of the mountain's wilderness experience.

The low winter sun will turn the high broad ridges, or the summit plateau of Mangerton, into a wonderland; a vast expanse of countless sparkling prisms. (Seán Ryan)

153

WINTER

Winter comes early and is prolonged. It is commonly the longest season in high mountains, sometimes twice as long as any of the others. Altitude lowers temperatures by about 1°C for every 150 m ascent. Up high the winds are much stronger and much more frequent, the rainfall even heavier and more prolonged, all of which severely restricts the growing period and the rate of growth. High mountains make their own weather; when the lowlands of Killarney are basking in the golden colours of an occasional balmy late autumn day, the high summits are often already dusted with snow. The first to carry snow are the highest summits of the Reeks.

The Irish name for the Reeks is *Na Cruacha Dubha*, or the Black Peaks. Whoever named them named them well. Black is their predominant colour, but what a variety of shades and tones: the black cliffs of Na Teanntaí reflected at evening in the silver stillness of Lough Callee; the water-saturated green-black sides of Com Úi Dhuibh, accentuated by late winter sunshine; the purple-black of cloud shadows on the north coums; but especially the deep mat blackness of the valleys far below, seen by climbers on a winter's evening from the summit snows.

The essence of the Reeks can be summed up as steep slopes and narrow ridges. Some of the ridges are very narrow and provide spectacular mountain scenery on a magnificent scale. Unfortunately they lie outside the park. There is nothing within the national park to compare with the knife-edged arête of An Barr Caol, from Caher to Carrauntoohil, especially in the snows of winter; nothing to equal the serrated rock pillars on the narrow cock's comb of the Beanncaorach – Carrauntoohil arête, or the even narrower saw-tooth arête from Cruach Mhor to Cnoc na Peiste. The snow plastered precipices and frozen waterfalls of the north faces of Carrauntoohil and Caher are unequalled within the park, especially in April when the sun's rays have climbed high enough to at last spill over the high rims and penetrate down into coums that have lain in deep shadow for months. The main ridge of the Reeks, sustained at above 900 metres, is both an exciting and wonderful experience in deep snow, when cornices curl out over the sheer north cliffs. In a blizzard or whiteout, it can be demanding, requiring experience and precise navigation.

Even in such extremes, life exists; on the surface of frozen summit snows lie many insects, mostly blown up by high winds. The ground is frozen iron

hard, yet deep within the iced-up and stunted vegetation lives a flightless insect life in its own world and micro-climate at ground level, insulated by the snows. Winter days are very short and frequently clouded, with showers of sleet and hail. This is the time to savour close up detail on the summits; each blade of sedge and grass is coated in pure crystal ice; mosses are furred with white hoar frost; snow drifts are fluted by the wind; sometimes hoar frost can cover the entire mountain range with a grey white fur; spikes of ice crystals grow out into the prevailing wind. A low winter sun will turn the high broad ridges, or the summit plateau of Mangerton, into a wonderland; a vast expanse of countless sparkling prisms.

These conditions, with air temperatures of –8°C to –10°C (but with wind-chill it feels about –30°C), are arctic-like, and it is one of the exceptional wilderness experiences of Killarney's high mountain systems that one can go from a valley floor environment with Mediterranean type vegetation, up to a true sub-arctic environment at 1,000 metres, in about three hours.

Plant and animal life must be specialised to survive these conditions. One of the larger year-round residents is the blue or Irish mountain hare. It is considered an endemic sub-species, which turns partially white in winter, very rarely turning all white like its more northern kin. It frequents the ragged lower edge of snow line, where the mixture of snow patch, brown vegetation and dark rock provides a perfect background for its piebald camouflage. A principal predator is the fox, whose tracks in the snow follow along the crests of the highest ridges up to 1,000 metres. Occasionally a flock of snow buntings comes visiting with a cold spell. Flying across a black cliff face, they resemble a flurry of snowflakes and are a magnificent, though rare, sight in the highest coum floors.

The low slopes may escape without snow cover, though not always. The colourful autumn grasses such as *Molinia* are now withered to a uniform whitish straw colour, its Irish name *fionán* being descriptive. Here the winter coat of the red deer blends exceptionally well with such lightish fawn colours; the black winter coat of sika deer stands out in contrast. In occasional years, heavy snowfall also accumulates on these lower slopes and valley bottoms; then the longer legs of the red deer provide a mobility which enables them to exploit both windswept ridges with exposed vegetation, or the lush pastures of the lowlands. Some of the large dominant stags, which ascended for the rut, now descend again to the lowlands and enjoy the luxury of rich limestone-based grasses in the winter. Many of the red deer remain on the uplands, where winter competition from sheep is very evident, especially on the green flushes termed locally 'inches' or 'pairceens', which are often grazed to the bare earth. The mountain-bred red deer can live out a harsh winter on a bare mountain side, and can be observed high up on the hard frozen slopes, even in the depth of winter. Greens are now much sought after. Heather and dwarf furze are an important standby. Slope aspect is also important, the warmer south and south-west facing slopes being favoured.

The mountain winters of Killarney National Park and adjacent ranges provide superb wilderness experiences of solitude and silence. Here one can be absolutely alone and in command of one's own survival. Everywhere there is a severe beauty; whether it be a waterfall blown back up a cliff face by the fury of a storm; the updraughted plumes of extremely fine powder snow smoking upwards and stinging like needles on the high tops, or the purity of a curve of virgin snow against a blue sky.

SPRING

Spring comes late to the high hills, the earliest signs are on the lowest slopes. One of the earliest is the tumbling flight of the black ravens above their nesting ledges, which may be occupied as early as February. By the end of March the wild geese have already left, and now the summer bird visitors arrive. One of the earliest is the wheatear, frequenting the boulder fields, and soon common sandpipers come back to the stony shores of the high lakes and streams, their piping calls an evocative sound of the great undisturbed silences.

Soon the meadow pipit, the mountains' most common bird, indulges in its short song and descending flight; its nest and chocolate brown eggs are hidden deep in the tussock vegetation. It is followed by the cuckoo, whose call echoes through the hills by early May; the Irish name for the meadow pipit is *giolla na cuaiche* (servant of the cuckoo). It is prey to both merlin and kestrel, two falcons which hunt and nest in the national park hills. The much larger peregrine falcon also nests in the park, and can now be heard calling shrilly, and wheeling, high over its nesting cliff sites. The vegetation begins to change, starting on the lower slopes. On the sheltered south-facing gullies of Torc, a few primroses appear, but later than in the lowlands. Two special flowers of the mountain spring are the Irish butterwort and the mountain saxifrage. The delicate sprays of pink flowers of the saxifrage, sunlit against dark rocks, are altogether more isolated and precious at 1,000 metres than at roadside level.

A meadow pipit (John J. Earley)

157

A wheatear.
(John J. Earley)

One of the earliest greens to appear is the yellow-flowered Irish spurge; it is poisonous, and though starved for greens, the deer will not touch it.
(Seán Ryan)

158

But spring comes later to the higher hills; it is mid-May before the new green growth of mountain grass pushes up through the white withered *fionán* of winter. One of the earliest greens to appear is the yellow-flowered Irish spurge; it is poisonous, and though starved for greens, the deer will not touch it. A late spring, especially after a prolonged severe winter, preceded by a wet summer, is the time when deer mortality reaches its peak on the hills. Ironically, some die off just as the first greens appear. It is a cull that is fundamentally different from the artificial selectivity of sport shooting which was practised on these hills for many years.

It is a wonderful time to walk the hills; you may find a cast antler, and savour the rushing sounds as mountain streams foam, swollen by flood rains and snow melt. Beneath the torrents of white water, the larvae of stone fly cling, flattened against water-smoothed rocks. On the heather-clad slopes, a walker will be lucky if a red grouse erupts close by and goes off with a clatter of wings and its famous 'go-back, go-back' call. It is a joy to watch flying low and quickly gliding along the curve of hill. Rarely does it settle within sight of a human intruder; it is a master of evasion. The Irish red grouse, once considered an endemic sub-species, is a true mountain dweller that lives out its life at high altitude. It is now rare in the park; shooting records tell of nearly 400 birds shot in the season of 1884; by the end of the Second World War, a season only yielded seven birds; today an observer would be lucky to count three or four in a full day's walk.

Life suddenly blossoms. With increasing temperatures, the sheep ticks, unwelcome parasites on hill walkers as well as sheep, become active; at about 300 metres badger tracks appear in certain areas of the park; the foxes are already scavenging in open daylight to feed their litters of cubs. On the highest tops some snow may yet remain, but by May the floors and sides of the high coums are already thawing, and reveal once more the fresh colour of rocks and stones. Suddenly a wren sings. The full appreciation of the beauty of its song is best experienced by those who hear it suddenly burst forth in the utter stillness of a high mountain coum, where it echoes and reverberates around the soaring walls of rock. Spring, at last, has fought its way to the high tops.

Conservation

When considering and assessing these mountains, it is desirable to consider that their wildlife doesn't have to be rare to be precious and important. Wildness itself is just as important; silence; the sense of open spaces and clear skies; the beauty of undefiled panoramas; a landscape of outstanding beauty that is world famous. These mountains, and particularly the highest land such as the Reeks, differ from other terrestrial ecosystems in that it is still possible to save them in an unspoilt and largely pristine state. They, and all our high mountains, are the last outposts of true wilderness, where one is a privileged visitor only. The national park hills have a particular importance in that they form the main range of the truly wild herd of indigenous red deer. Nowhere else in Ireland have red deer survived with an unbroken line stretching back to prehistoric times.

Even such critical areas, however, are not without threat, and some damage is already evident. Particularly regrettable and unwelcome is the practice of motorcycle scrambling on the national park hills and on the nearby mountains. Apart from flouting national park regulations, it results in the dispersion of wildlife outside the protection of the park, vegetation is damaged by the criss-cross of ruts and erosion channels, and the traditional tranquillity and natural beauty of Killarney itself is destroyed. In the nearby mountains which flank the park, there is also the increasing threat of commercial development, especially in the proliferation of mountain hydro-electric schemes. The development of one such, in Coumloughra in the Reeks, included the excavation of an access road, with cuttings up to four metres deep in places. It was a rape of one of the most pristine high mountain coums left in the country.

Some of Killarney's business community have already publicly stated the desire and intention of placing cable cars on the park's mountains. It would be difficult to envisage a greater act of vandalism to the beauty of Killarney and its national park. The very essence of Killarney's mountain scenery is clear, clean, rugged outlines against uncluttered and unpolluted skies.

Of the estimated one million tourists who visit Killarney each year, only a tiny fraction venture into these mountains, a situation unlikely to continue. There is a real need, therefore, while these mountains are still unspoilt, for the national park to establish a human activity carrying capacity which would not seriously damage the mountains' ecology. The fragile ecosystems of the mountains can be seriously and severely damaged by over-use and ignorance.

The mountains of Killarney National Park comprise about one-sixth of the mountains of the Greater Killarney Area, but they are an important part, as the park provides some measure of protection at present. Outside its boundaries lie the magnificent mountain groups of Lough Guitane, the Reeks, Clounlough/Lough Derriana, and the Coumasaharn complexes. All of these are more exposed to exploitation, as they do not yet enjoy the protection of a national park.

Perhaps some day they will.

(Since this was written substantial mountain areas of Kerry have been given protection as proposed Special Areas of Conservation under the EU Habitats Directive.– Ed.)

Important Warning!

The Kerry mountains are regularly underestimated. Since 1966, when records began, 35 people have been killed in the mountains, seventeen of whom died in the Reeks. People venturing into these mountains should be aware of the dangers common to all mountain country, and should seek advice from a recognised mountaineering organisation.

Chapter 10

The Woodlands

Daniel L. Kelly

Introduction

The woodlands of Killarney make this a place apart. We have here not just a wood, or a series of woods, but a whole wooded landscape. Through all the vicissitudes of the past centuries, the woods of Killarney have persisted; and today they contain the largest area in Ireland that is still dominated by the species of the primeval forest.

These woods are remarkable also for their diversity. Nearly all of the different types of woodland to be found in Ireland are represented within these few square kilometres. Responding to the ecological influences of soil type, rainfall and human activity, the Killarney woodlands form a patchwork of different woodland types: swamp woodlands, yew woodlands, oak woodlands and plantations of a range of deciduous and coniferous trees. In some areas the patches are large, such as in Tomies wood or Derrycunihy where a few hundred hectares of oakwood can be found. In other areas the patches are much smaller, such as on the Muckross Peninsula, where it is possible to pass from swamp woodland, through yew wood into oak wood in a few minutes' walking.

If we examine any one of these woodland types we will find yet another patchwork on a smaller scale. Mosses and other plants of the forest floor may change over distances of a few metres or even centimetres. In the Muckross yew wood, if you walk slowly deeper into the wood from the bright, windy, clifftop edge, you will quickly pass from grass, heather and furze into areas dominated by mosses. Take a close look at these mosses before you proceed further into the wood. When you reach the deepest, darkest part of the wood, you will observe that the woodland floor is carpeted with noticeably different types of moss, of which the tallest is called *Thamnobryum alopecurum*. With its stiff stem and clustered dark green branches at the top, *Thamnobryum* looks like a miniature palm tree or feather duster. This pattern of vegetation change from the edge to the middle of the wood is repeated on an even smaller scale. If you examine some of the narrow crevices in the limestone close to the edge of the wood, 20 cm down in the crevice you will find the same species as you found deep in the wood.

All of these variations in the woodland are orchestrated by variations in the environment. In areas with great environmental diversity there is a corresponding diversity in the vegetation. Minor themes in the environmental orchestration are the degrees of exposure to or shelter from wind and light, which in turn influence the air humidity, and these factors may produce variation in vegetation from one side of a rock to the other. However, in Killarney the major theme is the great variety of soils. Soil type is determined primarily by the nature of the underlying rock. A major geological divide separating limestone areas from sandstone areas occurs in Killarney, giving rise to two very different soil zones with their associated types of woodland. There is also variation in vegetation in relation to soil depth. In some areas the bedrock comes right to the surface, in others it is overlain by several metres' thickness of glacial deposits or peat. As well as variation due to underlying rock type and soil depth there is variation in relation to soil moisture. Some areas are subject to waterlogging or even flooding, whilst others are always well-drained. So, although there are many different ways of classifying woodlands, perhaps the most straightforward way to classify the different kinds of woodland at Killarney is on the basis of soil conditions.

The Woods on Sandstone

The Old Red Sandstone weathers to yield a strongly acid soil, poor in nutrients, just a thin skin of raw humus over a mixture of sand and stones.

If you travel through the Killarney Valley along the road to Kenmare or by boat along the Long Range river and through the Upper Lake, the woods which you can see skirting the lower slopes of the mountains and sometimes stretching in narrow gullies towards the higher ridges are the woods on sandstone. If you have time to leave the road or river, you will discover

Woods on sandstone in the park are dominated by oak though other native tree species are also present such as yew, ash, rowan, birch, alder, hazel and aspen. This aspen tree stands out in the autumn among the oaks on the shore of Glena. (Bill Quirke)

165

that the woods on sandstone are by no means uniform. They vary from high forest to low scrub; some areas are steep and rocky, others relatively level. There is also a marked gradient in rainfall. The annual rainfall in the vicinity of the Upper Lake is almost twice that at Killarney town, so the woods around the Upper Lake are much moister than Tomies Wood on the western shores of Lough Leane or Camillan Wood on the Muckross Peninsula. So, as we move southwards through the Killarney valley to the higher rainfall areas, there is a marked increase in the diversity and luxuriance of the mosses and liverworts. The filmy ferns with their small, delicate, translucent fronds only two cells in thickness also become more abundant. Two filmy fern species (both of the genus *Hymenophyllum*) are common on rocks and tree trunks in the higher-rainfall woods.

As well as this variation from one part of the sandstone woods to another, a variation in environment and vegetation can be seen in the vertical dimension, between the ground and the treetops. Here the dominant environmental themes are light and moisture. The first thing you will notice is that the trees seem to grow in two distinct layers. The top layer or canopy is composed of trees 13–20 m high (reaching 25 m in some places), and the lower layer or understorey is made up of small trees and large shrubs. The canopy is composed of deciduous trees, mostly sessile oak (*Quercus petraea*), which thrives on these poor, acid soils. Few of the oaks are of great age; this will be understood when you read in Chapter 3 of the traumas that the woods have undergone in recent centuries. Perhaps the finest surviving stand of tall oaks is in Derrycunihy Wood close to the site of the now vanished Queen's Cottage.

The understorey is composed largely of holly. To a visitor from continental Europe one of the most unusual features of these woods is the abundance of broad-leaved evergreen trees. This is especially striking in winter, when the canopy trees are bare, and the sunshine makes the glossy leaves of holly and ivy glitter. Another evergreen tree, arbutus, also known as the strawberry tree from its scarlet fruits, is common on rocky outcrops and at woodland margins. It is rare elsewhere in Ireland, absent from Britain, reappears in the west of France, and finds its main distribution in the Mediterranean region. The abundance of broad-leaved evergreens in the west of Ireland is a reflection of the mildness of the winters – the trees of central

Europe are almost all either broad-leaved deciduous species or needle-leaved conifers. Introduced broad-leaved evergreens do remarkably well in Killarney. Among these the common rhododendron, *Rhododendron ponticum*, introduced in the nineteenth century, has become a serious pest, having completely taken over the understorey in many parts of the woods (see Chapters 5 and 12)

It is in the tree layers that we find one of the most remarkable and beautiful features of these woods. The trunks of most of the trees at Killarney have their bark more or less concealed by the growth of mosses, liverworts, lichens and filmy ferns. The larger boughs of oaks and other trees are covered in a thick green carpet of moss, from which sprout the fronds of the polypody fern. The smaller branches are covered by glossy purplish mats of the liverwort *Frullania tamarisci*. Minute pitcher-like lobes on the undersides of the leaves of this plant help it to conserve water during dry spells. The lichen *Lobaria pulmonaria* (tree lungwort) is conspicuous on both trunks and branches, changing when wetted from grey to vivid green. This species, like many of Killarney's lichens, is highly sensitive to atmospheric pollution; it is an indicator of air that is clean as well as moist. A few flowering plants grow perched in tree-forks or on low mossy boughs, especially in the higher-rainfall woods, and even young saplings of mountain ash and holly can be seen growing on the moss-covered branches of larger trees. All these smaller plants which grow perched upon larger plants, but without extracting any nutrition from the larger plant, are known as epiphytes. The advantages of their perched position lie in the greater access to light and the reduced levels of competition from other plants. Lack of light limits the growth of smaller plants in a wood, especially in summer when the foliage of the canopy trees forms a dense screen. A disadvantage of this way of life is that epiphytes have no contact with the soil, and so their water supply is precarious. They are characteristic of regions where moisture is plentiful at all seasons. A profusion of epiphytes is characteristic of moist tropical forests. A number of closely related species – for example species of *Hymenophyllum* (filmy ferns) and of *Frullania* (liverworts) – are found in both the montane rain forests of tropical regions and the 'temperate rain forest' of Killarney.

As well as the two tree layers, if you look beneath the shade of the trees and shrubs, you can distinguish two further layers in the woodland vegetation: a

The trunks of most of the trees at Killarney have their bark more or less concealed by the growth of mosses, liverworts, lichens and filmy ferns. The multiple trunks of this oak provide evidence of coppice management in past centuries. (Daniel Kelly)

layer made up of flowering plants and ferns known as the field layer, and the moss layer. The field layer is rather sparse in these woods, and has relatively few species. The commonest members are hard fern, great woodrush and bilberry or fraughan, a small shrub with edible blue berries; all three species are characteristic of strongly acid soils. The field layer is kept down by the very heavy grazing pressure by deer and sheep. Whilst tree seedlings are plentiful from time to time, they invariably succumb to grazing. Saplings and young trees are

Spring growth before the woodland canopy casts its deep summer shade: fern fronds unfurling. (Padraig O'Donoghue)

169

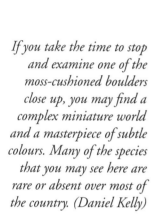

If you take the time to stop and examine one of the moss-cushioned boulders close up, you may find a complex miniature world and a masterpiece of subtle colours. Many of the species that you may see here are rare or absent over most of the country. (Daniel Kelly)

conspicuous by their absence. This lack of tree regeneration raises ominous questions for the future of the woods (see Chapter 12).

In contrast to the field layer, the moss layer is remarkably luxuriant and rich in species. All around you, boulders and tree trunks are padded out by a thick cushion-like covering of mosses and leafy liverworts. Because of their small size it is easy to overlook the wonderful diversity of mosses and liverworts, and this may be the reason that most of them have no common names. But if you take the time to stop and examine one of these moss-cushioned boulders close up, you may find a complex miniature world and a masterpiece of subtle colours. Many of the species that you may see here are rare or absent over most of the country.

The Woods on Limestone

The Carboniferous limestone weathers to produce a much more fertile soil, rich in calcium. Around Killarney the limestone is confined to the lowlands, and is largely concealed beneath a mantle of glacial soil. Nearly all the land with a continuous layer of glacial drift was cleared of forest centuries ago and converted to agricultural use.

Around Lough Leane and the Middle Lake the limestone bedrock comes close to the surface, and there are substantial areas of native woodland. The Muckross Peninsula and Ross Island are areas of remarkable biological diversity, with an alternation of craggy ridges, dense thickets, open glades and low marshy hollows. Heading out cross-country in a particular direction, one may have the disconcerting experience of finding that one has in fact walked in a complete circle! It is worth the risk as the flora of these areas is exceptionally rich.

The Muckross Peninsula has considerable stretches of tilted 'limestone pavement', scored by deep vertical fissures (known as grikes). This is the terrain that characterises the famous Burren region of County Clare. Unlike the Burren, the Muckross limestone is almost entirely covered in woodland. The principal tree is the yew, a tree whose roots show a remarkable ability to penetrate into crevices in solid rock. This is the only yew wood in Ireland, and one of the very few in western Europe. Yew is famous for its longevity; however the yews of this wood are not of a great age. Counts of annual growth rings on a number of dead trees found that the oldest, a very large specimen, was only about 200 years old. Probably the oldest yew at Killarney is the well-known specimen at Muckross Abbey. It was already a remarkable tree by 1756, when Charles Smith described it thus: 'one of the tallest yew trees I have ever seen; its spreading branches, like a great umbrella, overshadow the niches of the whole cloister.'

The evergreen yew wood canopy is low, generally 6–14 metres. There is no distinct understorey, though hazel and holly become frequent locally. The field layer is sparse; however, it has increased markedly in recent years through changes in the pattern of grazing in the Muckross area. The moss layer is strikingly well developed, clothing the limestone rock in a thick green blanket. There is virtually no soil except in the grikes and hollows.

Limestone areas with a continuous soil cover support tall trees and a different flora. This is the woodland type richest in spring-flowering herbs, especially those arising from an underground bulb or tuber: bluebell, wood anemone, wild garlic, pignut and lords-and-ladies or cuckoo-pint (*Arum maculatum*). In spring these woods are carpeted with bluebells and snow-like drifts of wild garlic flowers. These 'vernal' species concentrate their growing and flowering in spring, before the canopy above comes into leaf and the shade deepens on the woodland floor. As summer advances, their leaves turn yellow, wither and soon disappear; all that is left above ground are bare stalks bearing the seed heads. Most stands of woodland of this type have clearly been planted with oak, beech or other species.

Fungi are a feature of all the Killarney woods and the woods on limestone are particularly rich. In a good autumn you can encounter a wide variety of toadstools on a short walk through the woods; toadstools of almost every conceivable colour, ranging from sooty black to gleaming white, through yellows, purples, pinks, greens and browns, as well as the dramatic red with white spots of the fly agaric (of fairy tale fame). The mushroom is

Limestone areas with a continuous soil, such as Clochmacuda Wood in Knockreer, are the woodland type richest in spring-flowering herbs. In spring these woods are carpeted with bluebells and snow-like drifts of garlic flowers. (Bill Quirke)

Close to the estate houses at Muckross and Knockreer, avenues and small plantations, such as this at Muckross, were planted to enhance the demesne landscapes. (Seán Ryan)

just a particular kind of toadstool: all are the spore-bearing structures of fungi. Most fungi are decomposers, organisms that bring about decay. They release the stored-up energy in dead leaves and dead timber; without them the wood would gradually choke in its own discarded 'litter'. Some of the toadstools in the Killarney woods are good to eat, for instance the chanterelle. At least one species, the death-cap, is deadly poisonous; however, it is not hard to identify and so to avoid. Many fungi live on rotting logs. Other species are parasites, invading the trunks of living trees. Birch is one of our most short-lived trees; at Killarney dead and moribund birch trees are common, bearing the white spore-bearing 'brackets' of the fungus *Piptoporus betulinus*. The spores enter a tree by the wound left where a branch has broken off and the fungus spreads from there into the heartwood.

The Wetland Woods

Extensive low-lying areas east of Lough Leane are subject to flooding in winter; in summer they dry out to varying degrees. The woodlands here are composed largely of alder, sally (*Salix cinerea* subspecies *oleifolia*, the commonest kind of willow in Ireland) and downy birch. During the long wet periods of winter the lake rises and spreads into these woods, submerging the woodland floor and leaving only the trees rising out of the water. This seasonal inundation must have a profound effect on the animal life of the woods. Many of the smaller animals must either move out or perish. However, red deer frequent the flooded woods and often move through the woods into the reed beds along the lake edge. In summer when the water recedes the wetland woods are transformed. The field layer is lush and rich in species, with sedges, grasses and rushes, and many flowers of marshy places, such as water mint, marsh bedstraw and meadowsweet. The moss layer is generally inconspicuous, but contains many distinctive species. The most extensive examples of these wetland woods are in the Ross Island, Reen and Knockreer areas of the national park.

Other wetland woods experience less fluctuation in water level. The spring-fed swamp around Cloghereen Pool is almost equally wet at any season. This swamp is characterised by massive tussocks of greater tussock sedge (*Carex paniculata*), with treacherous pools between. A senior member of the park's management is rumoured to have vanished up to his armpits into one of these pools, so be warned! Another remarkable swamp is situated just west of the road between Muckross village and Torc waterfall; the site is flooded for much of the year, and the alder and sally trees have developed stilt roots from the trunks. This is a feature typical of tropical swamp forest, but unusual in western Europe.

Conifers

Yew – not a conifer in the strictest sense – and juniper are native to the region. Juniper (the shrub whose blue 'berries', actually modified cones, give flavour to gin) is sparsely distributed, mainly on the lake islands and lakeside rocks. Scots pine was a major component of the prehistoric forests, but apparently died out in the region around 200 AD (see Chapter 5). This was the first conifer to be planted in Killarney on a significant scale, starting from about 1800. Once reintroduced, the species has thrived; it is now regenerating freely around the shores of Muckross Lake.

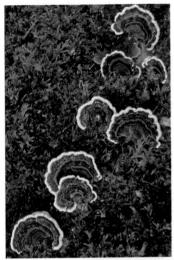

Fungi in the Muckross yew woods. (Pascal Sweeney)

The Killarney region includes extensive tracts of planted conifers, mainly species of spruce, pine and larch. Other species were inserted into the pre-existing woods as ornamentals, singly or in small stands; for instance, the enormous Monterey pines on the Muckross Peninsula. Most of the conifer plantations were planted within the past 75 years, and have only a very impoverished flora.

175

Extensive low-lying areas east of Lough Leane are subject to flooding in winter; in summer they dry out to varying degrees. These support a distinctive wetland wood community.
(Seán Ryan)

Animal life in the woods

The Killarney woods contain a diversity of furred and feathered life, but most of it will be seen only by those who are prepared to go quietly and wait patiently. If you take a ramble through one of Killarney's native woods on a calm summer day, at first everything will seem wonderfully silent, as if there was nothing living in the wood except the trees and slowly growing mosses. In fact, you are surrounded by a greater variety of life than you will find in almost any other place in the country. Sit for a while with your back to a tree trunk and listen and watch. Soon you will hear the sound of birds feeding in the tree canopy: tits, tree-creepers and goldcrests searching for the innumerable insects that feed on the trees; in the branches and on the ground, blackbirds, chaffinches and thrushes foraging; if it is early summer, the cuckoo calling.

Gradually the profusion of smaller creatures will become apparent: the subliminal hum of thousands of insects in the canopy; the shafts of sunlight criss-crossed by flying insects. Look closely at a handful of dead leaves, break off a piece of rotting wood, or look under a layer of moss and more life is

The spring-fed swamp around Cloghereen Pool is almost equally wet at any season. This swamp is characterised by massive tussocks of greater tussock sedge (Carex paniculata) with treacherous pools between. (Daniel Kelly)

Another remarkable swamp is situated just west of the road between Muckross village and Torc waterfall; the site is flooded for much of the year, and the alder and sally trees have developed stilt roots from the trunks. This is a feature typical of tropical swamp forest, but unusual in Western Europe. (Daniel Kelly)

revealed. If you are lucky, you may encounter a red squirrel or a red or sika deer. The mammals of the woods are shy and wary, but often you can observe the signs of their presence: ivy and holly leaves browsed away up to 1.2 metres from ground level show that deer feed in the wood; badger setts with discarded bedding at the entrance show that their owners are at home; foxes, pine martens, field mice, voles and shrews all leave some indication of their presence: droppings, footprints or pieces of hair.

As with the plant life of the woods, the different animals are adapted to different conditions and ways of life. Simply finding food is a dominant pre-occupation of all animals and we can divide the woodland animals into feeding types such as grazers, seed and fruit eaters, carnivores and insectivores.

Grazing animals

The only sizeable grazing animals that are a natural component of the woodland ecosystem are the native red deer and hares. Red deer frequent all the areas of woodland in Killarney except those that are densely infested with rhododendron. However, the extent of red deer usage varies greatly between different areas. The woods east of Lough Leane shelter significant numbers of red deer throughout the year. In Britain and Ireland red deer, though originally animals of the lowland forests, are now largely confined to poor mountain land. Here in the lowland woods of Killarney we have truly wild deer living in something close to their original optimal habitat. The native herbivores have been supplemented by a number of introduced species. The Japanese sika deer, introduced in the nineteenth century, is now widespread and numerous in the woods. Trespassing sheep are all too frequent, especially in the western woods of the park. Feral goats are also present, especially on Torc mountain. The impact of heavy grazing pressure on the woods is discussed further in Chapter 12.

Seed-eaters and fruit-eaters

Many of the trees and most of the shrubs at Killarney produce fruits which are eaten by animals. Many produce succulent fruits that are brightly coloured to attract consumers. The typical fruit-eater digests only the juicy pulp. The tough-walled seeds pass through unharmed, and will probably be deposited some distance from the parent plant; the animal thus acts as a 'dispersal agent' for the plant. At Killarney thrushes are major consumers of the berry-like fruits of holly and yew.

Seeds represent a much more concentrated food source, rich in calories and protein. The large seeds of nut- and acorn-bearing trees are important foods for woodland animals. In late autumn, when the acorn crop is heavy, the oak canopy is alive with the cooing and clattering of woodpigeons. The harsh cry of the jay is another characteristic sound of oakwoods. Jays became very scarce in Ireland in the nineteenth century, and have only reappeared in the Killarney woods in recent decades. The jay will fly off with an acorn or nut in its beak and then bury it, often at a considerable distance. A study in Germany found that on average each bird carried off 4,600 acorns in one season! Most of the seeds that get carried off will be eaten, but a few will remain unclaimed, and so will have a chance to germinate far removed from the parent tree. In spring, the jay turns its skills to carrying off eggs from the nests of other birds. Of the seed-eating mammals, the red squirrel is quite

The lowland woods to the east of Lough Leane shelter significant numbers of red deer throughout the year. (Paudie O'Leary)

easily seen, whisking up a tree trunk or bounding gracefully from branch to branch. It feeds mainly on nuts and on the seeds of conifers. The most numerous mammal in the woods is the field-mouse (*Apodemus sylvaticus*), but it is seldom seen as it is almost entirely nocturnal. It is easily distinguished from the house mouse (*Mus musculus*) by its white undersides, longer tail and larger eyes and ears. The diet of field-mice and voles in the Killarney woods has been studied in detail. In the yew wood, on the Muckross Peninsula, was found the highest densities of field mice ever recorded anywhere in the world. Seeds are the preferred food of the field-mouse; it is a major consumer of acorns and the seeds of holly and yew. Field mice are agile climbers: in the early autumn they frequently climb holly trees and extract the seeds from the still-unripe fruits. In spring and early summer, when seeds and fruits are scarce, insects become the chief food – mainly grubs and caterpillars. The bank vole, a rotund little rodent, was only discovered in Ireland in 1964, in the north of County Kerry; it is almost certainly a recent introduction. Now well-established in the Killarney woods, it differs from the field-mouse in being almost entirely vegetarian.

The quantity of seeds borne by many tree species varies enormously from one year to the next. In nut- and acorn-bearing trees a year of heavy bearing is known as a mast year. 1971, 1975, 1984 and 1995 were mast years for the oaks of Killarney. In the winter of 1971 the woodland floor was heaped with drifts of acorns. In some of the intervening years, you could search a whole wood and scarcely find a single acorn. For the seed-eaters, it may be either a feast or a famine. A good seed crop boosts breeding and overwinter survival in both field-mice and bank voles.

Carnivores

Whilst the herbivores have been augmented, the carnivore component of the fauna has been depleted through human activity.

Wolves were plentiful all over Ireland up to the seventeenth century. They were exterminated through forest clearance and the activities of bounty hunters. A publication of as late as 1690 refers to the wilds of Kerry as a haunt of wolves; they appear to have been extirpated from the county by about 1710. Golden eagles were still one of the sights for the eighteenth-century

Yew trees dominate the woodland which grows on the limestone pavement of the Muckross Peninsula. Their berries are an important food source for birds and small mammals. (Pascal Sweeney)

visitor to Killarney. They were gradually hunted to extinction in Ireland in the course of the nineteenth century, through the efforts of gamekeepers, shepherds and egg-collectors.

The carnivores of Killarney today are the smaller species. The fox is common, as everywhere in Ireland. Stoats are not common in the woods, probably because their principal food supply is rabbits, which are to be found mainly in the grassland areas of the park. The pine marten, today the rarest of Irish mammals, was reintroduced in the national park in recent years and now appears to be widespread in the park. The typical bird-of-prey of the woods is the sparrowhawk, a master of manoeuvre as it dashes between the trees after small birds. The principal predator of the nocturnal field-mouse is probably the long-eared owl, which emerges to hunt at dusk from its daytime roost in an evergreen or ivy-clad tree.

Insectivores

Many birds and mammals feed on invertebrates – animals without backbones, such as insects, worms and slugs. By day, the woods are never silent from the piping of small birds as they scour the trees in their incessant search for insects. Bird life in the woods is easiest to observe in winter, when the canopy is bare. Parties of long-tailed tits, coal tits, great tits, blue tits and goldcrests flit from branch to branch. The tree creeper jerks its way methodically up the trunk, probing the bark for hidden morsels. Landing near the base, it moves up the tree in a spiral, sometimes venturing onto the thicker branches; it then dives down to the base of the next tree to repeat the performance. The populations of these small birds fluctuate greatly, especially of goldcrest and long-tailed tit; they may be decimated by a harsh winter and their numbers may take several years to recover. In spring, the year-round residents are joined by more insect-feeders, back from their winter in Africa. The woods are enlivened by the call of the chiffchaff, the song of the willow-warbler and the aerial gymnastics of the spotted flycatcher.

The brown, marbled plumage of the elusive woodcock is a perfect camouflage against the dead leaves of the woodland floor. You rarely see it until you are very close, whereupon it takes flight with startling suddenness, zigzagging off through the trees. At dusk the birds leave the woods to feed in the open, probing soft ground with their long bills. Earthworms are their

Young sparrowhawks at the nest. (Paudie O'Leary)

182

staple diet, with some insect grubs and beetles. This was an important game-bird; 1,250 woodcock were shot on the Muckross estate in the winter of 1863–64. The rides in Tomies wood were kept open for woodcock shooting up to the 1930s.

Among mammals, the principal insect-eaters are bats, which catch insects on the wing, and hedgehogs and pygmy shrews, which hunt at ground level. Insects also form a significant part of the diet of many animals that are primarily seed-eaters (such as the field-mouse) or flesh-eaters (such as the fox).

The invertebrate fauna

The most numerous and least investigated animals of the woodlands are the invertebrates. Uncounted thousands of invertebrate animal species inhabit the soil, dead wood, bark and living vegetation of the woods. Any attempt to give them space proportional to their numbers would expand this chapter into many volumes!

The oak, in particular, supports an enormous diversity of leaf-munchers and sap-suckers: caterpillars, weevils, sawflies, mirid bugs, leafhoppers, greenfly, gall-wasps, gall-midges and so forth. Some years ago, in early summer, substantial areas of the oak wood took on a sadly dilapidated look. On closer examination the trees were seen to be partially or completely defoliated by the tiny caterpillars of the green oak moth (*Tortrix viridana*). On a still day, the frass or droppings falling from the thousands of caterpillars sounded like the pattering of fine rain on the woodland floor. Such infestations occur from time to time and provide rich feeding for the foraging birds of the woodland canopy. The trees normally compensate rapidly by putting out a flush of new foliage. Probably the tree most subject to dramatic insect attack is the sally; by July it is often an autumnal brown, due to the activities of leaf beetles. The grubs eat all but the lower epidermis, reducing the leaf to a skeleton; the adult beetles spread the damage further, often riddling the leaves with holes.

The tiniest caterpillars live inside the leaf, sandwiched between the upper and lower epidermis: they chew away at the green tissue, creating empty translucent patches known as leaf mines. Other mines, such as the brown

A wood ant nest.
(Bill Quirke)

blotches so common on the glossy leaves of holly, are caused by the grubs of small flies. Galls are distinctive growths or swellings produced by plant tissues in response to the presence of an internal parasite, usually an insect grub. The undersides of oak leaves are often decorated with small button-like growths; these are spangle galls, caused by the grub of a tiny relative of the wasp.

The speckled wood is the commonest butterfly of woods and shady places. This species shows a 'territorial' behaviour. An individual will take up a position in a sunny glade, basking watchfully, and flying off from time to time to make a circuit of its glade, as though on patrol. When another speckled wood flies into its territory, the 'defender' will dart up to challenge the 'intruder', and the two may engage in a harmless tussle. The silver-washed fritillary is a fast-flying species that is conspicuous on flowers in woodland glades. The caterpillar feeds on the leaves of violets. The purple hairstreak is a rare species typical of old woodlands; the caterpillar feeds on oak leaves, and the adult spends much of its time high up in the canopy – to the frustration of entomologists!

In some of the less frequented woods of the park you may encounter a two-way stream of large brown ants scurrying through the moss and rocks. In one 'lane' of traffic many of the ants can be seen carrying twigs, pieces of dead grass and dead insects. If you follow this direction along the ant highway, sometimes for up to 30 metres, you will eventually find an ant hill resembling a miniature haystack, constructed of tiny twigs and other woodland debris. These ant hills may be almost half a metre high and penetrate a similar distance under the ground, and a single ant hill may contain tens of thousands of individual ants. Wood ants *(Formica rufa)*, which construct these hills, are the largest species of ant in Ireland. The species has a curiously restricted distribution in this country.

A vital distinction between managed and natural woodland is that, in the latter, trees are allowed to go through the natural cycle of maturation, senescence, death and decay. The fallen tree is let lie. The presence of rotting timber, so offensive to the forester, is essential to the survival not only of many fungi, but also of a significant component of the invertebrate fauna. Decaying logs and stumps are tunnelled by the grubs of longhorn beetles or 'timbermen'; the adults are fairly conspicuous insects, sometimes seen feeding at flowers. Old standing trees commonly have rot-holes; the wet rotting wood provides a habitat for the grubs of certain hover-flies, including a number of rare species. Wood-inhabiting insects are the natural prey of woodpeckers but, sadly, there are no woodpeckers in Irish woods today. The great spotted woodpecker was apparently once part of the resident fauna, and still turns up from time to time as a winter visitor. It would seem that both woodpeckers and their insect prey have suffered as a result of the catastrophic decline in woodland cover and especially in the numbers of old trees in Ireland. Many insects of old woodland have diminished greatly all over Europe as modern silvicultural management has deprived them of their habitats. The national park thus has a particular importance in sheltering these threatened components of the woodland ecosystem.

The insects of the Killarney woods that most impose themselves on the attention of the public are the biting midges, or 'no-see-ums' as the Americans call them. Less than two millimetres long, dull grey with mottled wings, they have an uncanny skill in finding sheltered places to bite: up one's sleeves, behind one's glasses, down to the roots of one's hair – it makes one's scalp itch just to think of them! They are very sensitive to the weather – on a bright, breezy summer's day you might not encounter a single one. A warm, still, humid, overcast afternoon is perhaps their ideal – they come in clouds, and the temptation to flee to the open mountainside may become irresistible. From May to October or even November, you are as well to carry midge repellent in order to enjoy the woods without distraction. Mosquitoes, so typical of rain forests in other parts of the world, are happily not a feature of the Killarney woods (although six different species have been recorded from the area).

One of the most celebrated members of the Killarney fauna is the Kerry slug (*Geomalacus maculosus)*. 'Maculosus' means spotted: the slug comes in two principal forms, one with white spots on a black background, the other with yellow spots on a brown background. The Kerry slug is found in the woods over sandstone but not over limestone. Mainly nocturnal, it is active in the daytime on rainy days. It grazes a wide range of lichens, mosses, liverworts and algae – all plants that are disdained by larger grazing animals. This species has a remarkable geographical distribution, being found only in south-west Ireland (Kerry and west Cork) and in northern Spain and Portugal. This shows a parallel with the distribution of certain flowering plants: thus Saint Patrick's cabbage (*Saxifraga spathularis*) and kidney-leaved saxifrage (*Saxifraga hirsuta*) – both present in the Killarney woods – are likewise found only in Ireland and the Iberian peninsula. We already noted that the arbutus is found nowhere between the west of Ireland and the west of France. The reason for the wide gaps in the ranges of such species has long been a matter of debate; no one theory is satisfactory to explain all cases.

The Killarney woods are complex, diverse, and in many ways unique. Each wood has a different history, and the effects of these differences on the flora and fauna have yet to be adequately explored. The Killarney woods continue to pose a host of unanswered questions.

Chapter 11

THE BOGLANDS

Terry Carruthers

If you enter the Killarney Valley on the road over the mountains from the south, your first wide panorama of the national park will be at the famous 'Ladies View'. Here the eye is struck by the wild beauty of the woods, lakes and mountains all set amidst great expanses of bog. Covering much of the mountains, and surrounding the woods, the Upper Lake and the Long Range river, bogs cloak the park in a multicoloured mantle, ever changing with the passing seasons.

But what are these bogs and why do they exist at all? First and foremost, bogs consist of over 80 per cent water, almost as much as milk. To walk across

Bogs cloak much of the park in a multicoloured mantle, ever changing with the passing seasons. (Seán Ryan)

187

a wet bog, gingerly stepping from tussock to tussock, can be a hair-raising experience. At every step the surface of the bog shakes for several feet around you; it is probably the closest you will get to walking on water. The second most important component of bogs is peat, or turf, as it is called in Ireland. Peat consists of the undecomposed remains of plants, and forms in areas where the soil is water-saturated for most of the year. In water-logged soil, where oxygen is scarce and light cannot penetrate, only very special decomposer organisms can survive, and these only operate at a very slow pace. Thus the rate of decomposition is much slower than in normal soils, and once material sinks well below the surface, decomposition ceases entirely, leaving peat.

Conditions were not always wet enough for bogs to grow in Killarney. If you look closely at one of the few old turf cuttings in the national park, you may notice tree stumps exposed at the bottom of the bog. These stumps are thousands of years old. They date back to the great mixed forests of pine and oak which covered most of the Killarney area until the climate became wetter about 5,000 years ago, favouring the growth of peat. Pine seeds could not germinate in the wet peat and so the forests declined. Many pine trees were engulfed by the fast growing bog, and their preserved stumps remain – relics of an ancient forest.

In Ireland there are two main types of peat bog: raised bogs, once common in the midlands, and blanket bogs, more common on mountains and along the western seaboard. Both types are rapidly becoming scarcer, due principally to commercial afforestation and mechanised peat harvesting. The Killarney valley is fortunate in having large areas of virtually untouched bogs, mainly blanket bog, but also some rarer intermediate types. The fact that so few of the bogs were cut for fuel is probably due to the abundance of more easily obtained wood, and the fact that the area has always been sparsely populated. The surviving untouched bogs are in the least densely populated and less accessible areas of the Killarney Valley.

Because the nutrients contained in dead plants and animals are locked up rather than being recycled by decomposers, bogs are very deficient in minerals. They depend for their supply of nutrients on the small amount that comes in on wind and rain. To survive in this harsh environment, plants need special adaptations. Most bog plants have an open network of living cells which allows for maximum strength with minimum use of tissue. This

saves energy and allows the plants to draw oxygen down to their roots in the airless, waterlogged peat. Many bog plants augment their mineral supply by trapping insects, and eleven species of insectivorous plants are found on Irish bogs, many within the national park. The butterworts and sundews are the most obvious examples to be seen on the Killarney bogs. They emit a sweet sticky substance which serves to attract and capture their hapless victims. Their leaves are covered with special glands that emit digestive enzymes, enabling the plants to break down their victims' bodies and absorb the nutrients. The most striking of the butterworts is the greater or large-flowered butterwort *(Pinguicula grandiflora)*, which has beautiful purple flowers in early June. It has been described by some as the most beautiful of native Irish flowers. It is very common all over the Killarney hillsides.

The main peat forming plants are the sphagnum mosses, of which many species are found in Killarney. They are composed of two types of cells; small living cells, and large dead cells which have tiny holes to allow water in. Thus they hold their own water reservoir, necessary during the summer when the bog surface dries out. These sphagnum mosses have the ability to swap hydrogen, one of their waste products, for nitrogen and other minerals which are present in minute concentrations in the water around them. They also produce an antiseptic substance which inhibits other competing plants and further slows down the rate of decomposition. During the First World War, sphagnum mosses were used as wound dressings, having the ability to absorb blood and sterilise wounds. Another adaptation of bog plants is small leaves to reduce their surface area and hence the drying effects of the sun and wind, particularly during summer. The leaves of heathers are quite tiny and strongly curved, with their stomata or air holes located on the protected inside of the curled-up leaf. In autumn many of the bog-dwelling plants draw their hard-earned minerals into the relative safety of underground storage organs. Examples of such plants are the bog cottons (genus *Eriophorum*) and the white-beaked sedge *(Rhynchospora alba)*, both of which turn a lovely golden colour in the autumn, as the green-coloured chlorophyll is broken down, allowing the other pigments to shine through.

Most of the plant growth, the trapping of insects and the storage of reserves takes place in the summer. Life on the bog mellows in the autumn, and a beautiful golden-brown hue washes over the landscape. This is one of the most delightful times of the year in Killarney. Being out and about on a warm autumn's day, with the sound of rutting red and sika deer reverberating about the hills, and the bogs awash with gold, is one of the highlights of the year.

Another sound haunts the ear in early October; that of the Greenland white-fronted geese that have just winged their way from their breeding grounds on the coastal marshes of Greenland, where winter has almost set in. These geese, that settle on the bogs of Killarney National Park after thousands of miles of flight, are drawn by the abundant food supply of the bogs. Their principal winter food is the bulbils of white-beaked sedge and bog cotton. These large grey and brown birds, with their white facial patch, orange bill and legs, and black-barred underparts, are probably our most handsome goose, and are the rarest sub-species of goose in the world. Their total world population numbers 29,000, approximately half of which winter in Ireland. The bogs of the Irish west and midlands were once their main wintering grounds. However, with drainage and development of our bogs, most of the geese have switched to feeding on farmland, particularly on the Wexford

Bog asphodel is common on the bogs of the park. (Seán Ryan)

Bog cotton draws its hard-earned minerals into the relative safety of underground storage organs during the winter. (Seán Ryan)

Life on the bog mellows in the autumn, and a beautiful golden-brown hue comes over the landscape.
(Bill Quirke)

slobs, where over two-thirds of our Greenland white-fronted geese now overwinter. The number feeding on boglands has declined dramatically. The small flock which winters in the Killarney Valley, numbering between twenty and thirty geese in recent years, is one of the few flocks left which still feed entirely on blanket bog. The Killarney flock is now the only substantial flock left out of seven which wintered in County Kerry in the early 1980s. Thus the continued conservation of this small flock is high on the list of priorities in the national park.

Greenland white-fronts are very vocal geese, particularly in flight, and the sight and sound of a flock coming onto a bog is very special. After arriving in the Killarney Valley, the geese forage mainly on the Oak Island or Gearhameen bogs to the south of the Upper Lake. These bogs have the highest density of their preferred food, the white-beaked sedge. The underground bulbils of the white-beaked sedge are quite small, averaging one or two centimetres in length, and most plants produce ten to fifteen bulbils each. The geese concentrate on those bulbils which grow in the wetter pools, and are thus easier to extract. As the winter progresses, and the available store of food

The Boglands

The bogs to the south of the Upper Lake have the highest density of white-beaked sedge, the preferred food of the Greenland white-fronted geese. (Bill Quirke)

The number of Greenland white-fronted geese feeding on boglands has declined dramatically. The small flock which winters in the Killarney Valley, numbering between twenty and thirty geese in most years, is one of the few flocks left which still feed entirely on blanket bog. (Seán Ryan)

193

is used up, the geese feed more and more on the other bogs in the Killarney Valley. They are very wary and easily disturbed by walkers, anglers or unusual traffic noise. It is known that too much disturbance causes undue stress and restricts feeding time, and ultimately affects their reproductive success.

The geese have an interesting relationship with the sika deer which also feed on the bogs. Sika will actively seek out geese if they are feeding on the same bog, working their way among the flock and eating any goose droppings they can find. Geese are inefficient digesters of food. Much of the food value of the nutrient-rich bulbils which the geese have extracted from the bog is passed through in a semi-digested form in their droppings. The geese do the gathering, digesting and parcelling, and the deer enjoy a nutrient-rich, and sometimes warm, snack! The association may be mutually beneficial, as the geese probably benefit through increased security from having the deer present. You might wonder, however, when you see a goose almost being pushed aside by a deer which has probably just spotted another titbit.

The sika make a lot of use of boglands, mainly in late winter and spring. On fine spring mornings in areas near heavy cover of forestry or rhododendron, it is not unusual to see up to twenty deer out on the bogs. This is a good time of year to see these deer, as they become more elusive once the heavy growth of summer begins.

The most widespread breeding birds on the bogs are meadow pipits, while snipe are locally common. Snipe have a wonderful display flight in summer. The male rises high over the bog, then with his outer tail feathers spread out, glides earthwards. The wind rushing through his tail creates a distinctive vibrating sound, called drumming. The Gaelic name for snipe, *an gabhrín roa*, 'the cry of the goat', reflects this noise more accurately. The breeding population of snipe is boosted in autumn by an influx of immigrants from the Baltic regions and Iceland. On some bogs it is not unusual to flush up to 100 snipe in a short distance. They seem to have a distinct preference for certain bogs, as one can walk across other areas and rise very few snipe.

Though the bogs in the national park are safe from the threats of turf cutting and commercial afforestation, they are not safe from the threat of peat erosion. This is a problem that can be seen in every mountain range in the country. Peat erosion starts as cracks and deep gullies in the higher mountain bogs. Once formed, these cracks and gullies become enlarged until all that is left are dried chunks of intact peat called 'hags'. Evidence of peat erosion can be seen on the national park mountains, particularly Mangerton. The reasons for peat erosion are not clear; it may be the result of overgrazing or human disturbance, a natural process or a response to climatic change.

The most dramatic form of peat erosion is a 'bog-burst' or peat flow. Robert Lloyd Praeger in his book, *The Way That I Went* graphically describes a bog burst near Killarney in 1896:

> It was on peat-covered hills near Gneevgullia, out to the north-east of Killarney, that there occurred, three days after Christmas of 1896, an extensive bog-burst that attracted much attention on account of the tragic circumstances accompanying it, a family of eight persons, their home, and their livestock, having been carried away and buried. . . . In certain conditions, the lower layers of a bog may become so highly charged with water that under pressure of the superincumbent mass they gush out at the lowest point of the floor, dragging the wreck of the more solid upper layers after them. If the bog be large and deep, a great flood of semi-liquid matter may be ejected: and should the slope below the point of ejection be steep, a devastating torrent may result. Unwise turf-cutting, by producing a high face without due preliminary draining, has been frequently the cause of these accidents. It was so in the case of the fatal Kerry case; the face of the turf-cutting gave way, and a vast mass of peat and water precipitated itself down the valley, the flood ceasing only when it entered the Lower Lake of Killarney, fourteen miles distant. When the flow finally died down, about a week after the outburst, a great saucer-shaped depression, at its deepest no less than forty-five feet below the former slightly convex surface, showed the amount of the extruded material.

A scientific study of the deepwater sediments of Lough Leane carried out in the 1970s found a mysterious layer of peat up to twenty centimetres thick, buried beneath twenty to 60 centimetres of normal lake sediment. This was the peat from the 1896 bog-burst which settled to the bottom of the lake over 100 years ago. Richard Hayward, in his book *In The Kingdom Of Kerry* describes his visit to the scene of a bog-burst on Mangerton four years after it occurred in 1940:

Our path led across what looked like some silent valley of the moon, a vast bog which had been entirely denuded of its covering of turf, and that stretched before us in a desolation of twisted bog wood, rough boulders and patches of stunted vegetation scattered in the wildest confusion over a floor of sand and drift gravel. I have never seen anything in my life that brought such a sense of devastation and utter loneliness.' 'Dambut, every river was brown for weeks,' said Hayward's guide, 'and the poor trout thought it was the end of the world.

Throughout most of Western Europe bogs have become a thing of the past, and in Ireland undisturbed boglands are becoming fewer and fewer. We have an international duty to protect as many examples of the remaining types as possible, before they are lost forever to cutting, drainage and afforestation.

Evidence of peat erosion can be seen on the National Park mountains, particularly Mangerton. (Seán Ryan)

Chapter 12

CONSERVATION ISSUES

Bill Quirke

The natural and historical heritage which we have today in Killarney National Park bears witness to the success of the policies adopted by the national parks service in the 1960s and espoused to the present time. The development of park policy, the expansion of the park area, and the underpinning of park policy with vital scientific research are described in Chapter 1. The many achievements and the countless tasks, too numerous to even list, that are carried out with diligence, skill and dedication by park management and staff rarely receive comment. It is the nature of conservation that the problem areas get most of the attention, and so it is with this chapter.

At the beginning of a new century Killarney National Park is faced with formidable challenges. Challenges such as the destruction wrought by trespassing livestock, rhododendron, fire and water pollution; managing increasing numbers of visitors; and achieving a legal environment in which its conservation objectives can be most successfully achieved. A vital step in confronting these challenges was taken with the publication of the park management plan in 1990. This plan documents the park resources, outlines park aspirations regarding a wide range of conservation issues, and most importantly firmly reiterates that the basic and overriding role of the national park is the conservation of wild nature.

Legal Protection and Commercial Developments

Despite these encouraging developments, the conservation objectives and aims outlined in the management plan remain only official aspirations, with no legal status. While the national park will soon have legal protection as part of a Special Area of Conservation (SAC), no legislation defining or enforcing the primary conservation status of Killarney National Park exists. An

A Place to Treasure

Unauthorised advertising in the National Park. Some see the national park as an underdeveloped resource. (Paudie O'Leary)

Privately run water buses now operate on the Lower Lake in the park, instigated as a result of a political decision, rather than as part of any park plan. (Bill Quirke)

198

examination of events in the national park over the last twenty years indicates that, in the absence of legal definition, the official objectives and principles framed in the management plan are subject to widely differing interpretations. Events have shown that in the absence of a legal framework important decisions can be influenced by political considerations, by commercial interests urging 'development', and by pressure groups sometimes urging the opposite.

In recent decades the park has come under pressure from commercial interests to allow exploitation of what these interests see as an underdeveloped resource. For some years it appeared to some observers that such pressures were yielding success, and the park authorities were in conflict with local and national conservation groups as a result of several controversial decisions. More recently the park authorities have formed a united front with conservation groups in opposing proposals for developments in and adjoining the park.

The first controversy to gain major public and media attention was the decision in 1987 to allow privately-run water buses to operate on the Lower Lake in the park. This was instigated as a result of a decision made at political

An 'underdeveloped' section of the Lough Leane shoreline adjoining the golf course. (Bill Quirke)

*Shore line 'improvement'
works in progress in Lough
Leane – part of the natural
zone of the park.*

'Improved' Lough Leane shore-line. (Bill Quirke)

level, in response to pressure for commercial tourist development, rather than as part of any park plan.

Another controversial development took place along the northern shore of Lough Leane where the national park adjoins a private golf course. Here a substantial area of natural shoreline, supporting a diverse community of plants and animals, including a belt of alder wood, was removed and replaced by an artificial shore line. This took place as part of the development of a golf course in 1990 and 1991. Exactly locating the park boundary can be a difficult task; however, all available maps indicate that much habitat damage took place within the national park. In 1993, with the agreement of the park authorities, approximately 200 mature alder trees were felled on a previously undamaged shoreline to open up viewing lines from the golf course.

In 1988 a decision in principle was made by the national parks authority to accept a proposal to have 90 acres of the national park, close to Killarney town, leased and developed as part of a golf course. This was to prove the most controversial decision ever made in Killarney by the national parks authority. Local conservationists objected to the proposal both in principle and because of the impact it would have on woodlands and wildlife. All of these objections were rejected by the national parks authority.

After about two years of opposition to the plan by local conservationists, the national parks authority announced that 876 acres of mountain land belonging to Coillte (the state forestry company) would be added to the national park at its southern edge, in exchange for the lease of land for the golf course. (Coillte, unlike its predecessors, is a company in which the state is the major shareholder.) The park authorities claimed that the deal as a whole would benefit the park and nature conservation. Though it was accepted by all that this land would be a desirable extension to the park, opposition to the proposal continued on the basis that a privately-controlled golf course in the national park was objectionable in principle; that the people of Killarney would be deprived of 90 acres of park land on their doorstep; and that the golf course development would have severe adverse effects on wildlife and woodlands in the park and in state-owned and private lands adjoining the park.

In the spring of 1992 the locations for the tees and greens of the proposed course were marked out. An immediate escalation of opposition took place when it was seen that eight greens, seven tees and several fairways were to be constructed in woodlands. Spokespersons for the national parks authority continued to hold that there would be minimal adverse effects on woodlands and no adverse effects on wildlife. At this stage the issue focused unprecedented media attention on the national park. A prolonged campaign by an alliance of local groups resulted in the balance of local public opinion being strongly against the proposed development. The proposal was turned down by the government a few days before a general election in November 1992. The reason given by the park authorities for this decision was the impact the development would have on woodlands adjoining the park. The national parks authority have now facilitated greater public access to the area; however, they have consistently declined to reverse their official acceptance of the principle of leasing parts of the national park for developments such as a golf course.

In more recent years the parks service (now part of the Department of Arts, Heritage, Gaeltacht and the Islands) seems to have moved to a more strict interpretation of its conservation role. This may be partly due to the fact that the National Parks and Wildlife (NPW) section of Dúchas now has responsibility for the designation and protection of natural heritage areas (NHAs) and special areas of conservation (SACs). While NHAs and SACs now have a legal basis, the nature conservation role of national parks still does not. In recent years National Parks and Wildlife ecologists have had a more direct role in conserving lands not under NPW ownership. NPW has now proposed the area of native woodland previously earmarked for golf-course development as part of an SAC, and in co-operation with local conservation groups, has successfully opposed a new proposal for a golf course development in these woods. The parks service and local conservation groups have also successfully opposed proposals for road developments in the national park. The need to define the park's role in a more formal way is nevertheless clearly highlighted by the fact that in 1995 the park authorities actively and successfully opposed the development of a golf course in woodlands adjoining the park, while five years earlier they were vigorously defending a proposal to develop a golf course in the same woods, which would also have involved the development of 90 acres of the national park as a privately-run golf course. Whether one regards the former or the latter stance as most appropriate, the remarkable, and some would argue unsatisfactory, range of interpretations of the park's role is clearly illustrated.

The Practical Challenges

The national park's need for legal protection is clear; however, it is of equal importance that aspirations expressed in the management plan be translated into detailed action plans. Four conservation challenges stand out, because they threaten the very habitats that clothe the landscape and support the unique wildlife of the park. These challenges are lake pollution (see Chapter 8), rhododendron, grazing and fire. A fifth challenge, which is already growing rapidly, is how to accommodate the increasing numbers of people seeking unspoiled wildness, without damaging the park, its wildlife, and the very wildness that the visitor seeks.

RHODODENDRON

If acid rain or some other form of pollution had destroyed much of the unique community of plants and animals in half the oak woodland area of

Rhododendron infested oakwoods at Glena. Though colourful in June, these woods are impenetrable and most of the natural plants and animals have died out beneath the strangling cover of rhododendron. (Bill Quirke)

Beneath the rhododendron it is so dark that virtually nothing can grow. No trees can regenerate thus condemning the woods to eventual extinction. (Bill Quirke)

204

Killarney; if this pollution had changed the nature of the soil, prevented the woods from regenerating, sentenced the trees to gradual decay and disappearance and now threatened the remaining woods with similar destruction, there would surely be an outcry, both national and international. The fact that this destruction is indeed being wrought, not by chemical pollution, but by biological pollution in the form of an alien plant, somehow deflects attention from the problem. For some it is unbelievable that such destruction could be caused by a 'mere' plant. For others, any plant must be in some way 'natural' and therefore 'OK'. However, rhododendron in Killarney is no more natural than baboons in the Burren. Rhododendron is the most serious conservation problem facing Killarney National Park. Introduced from Turkey in the nineteenth century, it has virtually no natural enemies in Ireland. Nothing eats it; it is thought to release a substance into the soil that inhibits other plants; it grows rapidly on poor acid soil and each flower can produce thousands of tiny wind-blown seeds. Most importantly, it grows over four metres high, and so thickly that very little light can get through and the plants of the forest floor die. Though mature native trees usually survive, no young trees can grow and so the old trees die without being replaced. Rhododendron is at present primarily a threat to the woodlands, but experience in other areas shows it can eventually spread thickly onto open mountain. Rhododendron has spread to all areas of native woodland in the park.

In 1973 an in-depth study of rhododendron in Killarney concluded that 'a critical stage has now been reached, and an effort now will save a great deal of extra work at a later date'. The situation 27 years later is indeed more grave. Areas described in the 1973 study as 'largely free of rhododendron' have since become severely infested. In the 1990 management plan the national parks authority set themselves the aim of eradicating rhododendron from 75 per cent of the woodlands in the park within twenty years. Successful eradication of rhododendron from an area of woodland is difficult to achieve. Cutting down the visible standing plants only marks the beginning of the process. After that the stumps must be dealt with, either by uprooting or by spraying the re-growth with herbicide. Countless thousands of tiny rhododendron seedlings which emerge in the years after the initial clearance must also be dealt with; if not, the wood will rapidly return to a state of serious infestation. So success can only be achieved by several

205

Conservation volunteers cleaning rhododendron from the oak woods. (Paudie O'Leary)

thorough coverages of a wood over a period of years, and subsequently by constant vigilance to ensure that no rhododendron plant is allowed to grow up and produce more seed in the wood. The objective of eradicating rhododendron from 75 per cent of the Killarney woods over the next ten years (by the year 2010) can only be achieved if the clearance programme is absolutely systematic and meticulous. Partial clearance leaving seedlings or some flowering rhododendron will in the long run be a waste of time.

At the time of writing (June 2000) approximately 28 per cent of the oak woods in Killarney National Park have been cleared and are being maintained clear of rhododendron by the Groundwork Conservation Volunteers. Groundwork have brought many hundreds of volunteers from all over the world to work in the Killarney woods every summer since 1981. For ten weeks every summer, approximately 25 volunteers come for a period of one or two weeks to work in the oak woods. Volunteers stay in the national park at Arthur Vincent House which was converted to provide hostel facilities, primarily for conservation volunteers. The Groundwork volunteer programme has been financially supported since its inception by the national parks authority.

In the last ten years a major programme of rhododendron clearance has been undertaken by national park staff and contractors engaged by the park authorities. Under this programme approximately 35 per cent of the oak woods in the park are now undergoing clearance. In June 2000 flowering rhododendron were again to be seen throughout much of this area. An urgent and concerted push is therefore needed now to deal with regrowth and seedlings. Otherwise the major effort and expenditure of the last ten years may be largely wasted, and much of the 35 per cent of the oak woods in which inital clearance has been carried out may be lost again to rhododendron.

A clearance programme will need to be initiated in a further approximately ten per cent of the oak wood area if the objective of 75 per cent clearance is to be met by the year 2010. However, the most important challenge in the next ten years will be in the 35 per cent of the oak wood area where the clearance process has already begun. If success is to be achieved in these areas, rhododendron seed sources will have to be eliminated and seedling regrowth removed. This will be a challenging undertaking; however, there are few conservation tasks in Ireland so vital and so urgent, as the survival of our finest remaining native forests hangs in the balance.

GRAZING

Grazing is a normal part of mountain and woodland ecosystems. Red deer have grazed the Killarney area for thousands of years. However, present levels of grazing animals are far in excess of the level sustainable by the natural ecosystems of the park. Grazing has been so heavy in the park in recent times that there has been virtually no regeneration of young trees in any part of the oak forest for at least 60 years. This means that any old trees that die or are blown down by storms are not replaced, and so the woods are gradually ageing and deteriorating. The animals primarily responsible for this destruction are domestic sheep, Japanese sika deer and feral goats.

Three sika deer were released in Killarney in 1865. Sika numbers in the area are now probably between 600 and 800. In the winter months in recent years as many as 2,000 sheep graze the woods and mountains of the park. Feral goats were until recently thought to be confined to the steep north face of Torc mountain, and to be a fairly stable population of about 50 animals.

Sheep have no place in a national park of this kind; they damage the mountain vegetation, compete with the red deer for food, and threaten the very survival of the woodlands in the long term. (Bill Quirke)

However, it is now known that the population is probably four or five times this number. Goats are now regularly seen in the Tower Wood to the south of Torc mountain and have succeeded in crossing the Long Range river and penetrating at least two kilometres into the western woods of the park.

Apart from preventing regeneration of trees, excessive numbers of grazers have a detrimental effect on the plants of the forest floor. Removal of plant cover and disturbance of the ground provides ideal conditions for rhododendron seeds to germinate, and rhododendron completes the vicious circle by providing ideal shelter for sika deer. Damage is not confined to woodlands, as mountain vegetation also suffers from overgrazing. Some mountain areas are so overgrazed that erosion has occurred. Overgrazing also poses a direct threat to the native red deer. Deprived of food in the sheep-grazed mountains and woods of the national park, many red deer must either lose condition or move out of the park onto private farmland, where they cause considerable damage to crops and are exposed to the danger of legal and illegal culling.

Drastic measures are needed to bring grazing in the park down to a sustainable level and keep it there. The number of sika deer removed by culling in recent years has been between 150 and 200 per year. This culling level, if sustained or increased, should halt or reverse the growth of the sika population. However, concerted action to reduce sika deer numbers is largely a waste of time if it simply provides more grazing for the sheep. Despite the concern of the park authorities, no effective action has yet been taken to reduce or eliminate the serious problem of trespassing sheep in the national park. Sheep have no place in a national park of this kind; they damage the mountain vegetation, compete with the red deer for food, and threaten the very survival of the woodlands in the long term. The 1990 park management plan favours the driving off of sheep by park staff, impoundment, and court action against owners in the case of persistent trespass. Whereas the driving of sheep may have some chance of success in the more accessible Torc/Mangerton deer range, it would be difficult or impossible to keep the inaccessible western woodlands clear of sheep by this method.

The strategy outlined in the management plan has not yet produced significant results. Fencing, though troublesome and an intrusion in a natural landscape, should be retained as a last option if other methods do not produce results soon. Except in special cases, fencing of individual woods should be avoided, because this would be unsightly and would interfere with the natural woodland ecosystem more than fencing the park boundary or major zones within the park. Fencing around the park's woodlands individually would in any case be excessively costly and difficult. The western area of the park contains the most inaccessible, ancient, and biologically-rich oak woods as well as the largest area of woodland that is now almost free of rhododendron; these woods are under more severe sheep grazing pressure than any other woods in the park. Grazing pressure in *Glaisín na Marbh* wood, the highest in the park, has left the steep woodland floor bare and eroding. Ten kilometres of sheep fence along the western park boundary would protect all the western woods and mountains of the park. To fence these woods individually would require at least 30 kilometres of fencing.

The number of red deer in the national park now stands at approximately 700. Conservation of red deer is a top priority in the national park. Conservation of these animals will have to involve controlling their numbers. Otherwise, in the absence of wolves, their natural predator now extinct in Ireland, red deer numbers will continue to grow until their habitat is seriously degraded and starvation brings about a reduction in their numbers. I believe that the first priority should be to remove all sheep from the park and remove all sika deer and feral goats or reduce them to low and manageable numbers. Once this has been achieved, the optimum level of red deer can be established and the population kept at that level. The main criterion for establishing the optimum number of red deer should be the number that can be supported in the park while still allowing woodland regeneration.

FIRE

Despite Killarney's notoriously wet climate, fire is a serious problem in the national park. Unlike some areas of the world, fire is not a natural feature of Killarney's mountain and woodland ecosystems. In spring, before the new season's growth, much of the mountain area of the national park is vulnerable to fire. Dead mountain grass, heather and gorse can fuel fires of frightening intensity, particularly in dry, windy weather. Fires which burn hundreds of acres occur frequently in the park. Disastrous fires burning thousands of acres may occur only once or twice in a person's lifetime, but several times in the lifetime of a tree. Fire scars on living and dead trees and charcoal deposits in the woodland humus show that fire is a recurring problem. In the long term, fire is gradually reducing the area of woodland, and destroying the scattered trees, bushes and small woodland clumps that characterise the most natural areas of the park.

In 1984 several thousand acres of the western section of the national park were burned. While mountain grass recovered quickly, heather showed very slow recovery. The fire destroyed or severely damaged woodland fringes, isolated pockets of woodland, and countless oaks and hollies growing along rivers. In some larger, more open woods, where heather was abundant, the fire burned into the interior of the forest, damaging the ground vegetation and frequently destroying the dried out layers of epiphytic mosses on the trunks and branches of the trees.

In dry spring conditions, conventional beating and back-burning methods of firefighting are frequently inadequate once a fire has taken hold. In 1991 an important step forward was made when, for the first time, a firefighting helicopter was called in to fight a fire that had got out of control. However, under very dry conditions with strong winds,

In 1984, several thousand acres of the western section of the National Park were burned. The fire destroyed or severely damaged woodland fringes, isolated pockets of woodland, and countless oaks and hollies growing along rivers. (Bill Quirke)

conditions may exist for a fire disaster on the scale of the 1984 fire. Under such conditions firefighters on the ground backed up by helicopter will not be sufficient to control a serious fire once it has gone beyond a critical size and speed of spread. This is most likely to happen with fires started in the evening or after dark. Under such circumstances a strategy of containment could be adopted, for which detailed 'fall back' plans are needed to confine fires using river lines, rocky areas of sparse vegetation, and back burning.

Successful fire control in the park is vital, as the alternative is an inexorable whittling away of Ireland's finest remaining native forests and an impoverishment of the upland flora and fauna.

MANAGING VISITORS

One of the most important objectives of Killarney National Park is to enable people to visit and appreciate the park in ways that are compatible with its primary conservation objectives. This dual mandate contains the central challenge of all national parks: the challenge to implement what many

211

people would regard as a contradiction. It is probably true that wild nature, natural ecosystems, solitude, natural beauty and unspoiled scenic landscapes would be most effectively conserved if people were discouraged or prohibited from entering the national park at all. However, to implement such a measure would hardly be possible or desirable in a national park, where a primary reason for conservation is to benefit the public both now and in future generations.

There will be an inevitable trade-off between the two objectives of conservation and visitor facilitation. However, as conservation is the overriding objective, it is clear that there must be a limit to the level of impact and visitor usage which can be accepted, even though such limits may never be reached in many areas of the park.

A management principle of fundamental importance will logically follow if this idea of the park as a limited resource is accepted. This could be called *the principle of minimising impact and maximising appreciation*. If only a limited level of impact is acceptable, the park's secondary objective of visitor appreciation will be best served by ensuring that this 'impact limit' is 'used up' in a way that will provide maximum appreciation and enjoyment of the park for the maximum number of people. 'Second rate' uses of the park that have a significant impact, but an insignificant trade-off in terms of the visitor's appreciation of the park, should be discouraged or prohibited. Fortunately and crucially, the activities which give maximum appreciation are usually the activities that cause the minimum adverse impact.

It has been argued that, as national parks are public land, they should be available for any recreational activity. This would make sense if recreational activities had no effect on each other or on the park. This of course is not the case; one motor-bike scrambler on a mountain will render the mountain useless to the wildlife watcher or the person seeking natural beauty and peace. Six people taking a helicopter tour over the park will have a similar adverse effect on even larger areas of the park. Since 1986 many visitors have enjoyed viewing Lough Leane from one of the new waterbuses, one of which towers more than twelve feet above the water and dwarfs all the traditional craft of the lake. However, these craft have a significant impact on the appearance and traditional ambience of Lough Leane and therefore on the experience of other visitors; their effects on wildfowl and fish have never been studied. It must be accepted that in the same way as certain activities are not appropriate in art galleries, historical monuments and great cathedrals, likewise certain activities are not appropriate in a national park.

So how can suitable activities be encouraged and facilitated? The best and most appropriate way of appreciating the national park is simply by walking. It is therefore important that walkers should be facilitated as much as possible. Firstly, the many visitors who confine themselves to their car or tour bus might be encouraged to be more adventurous. Good interpretation facilities could help visitors to make the first steps towards encountering the park in reality, rather than acting as a substitute for reality. Visitors might first be directed to less demanding short walking trails. In addition to the already existing nature trails, a few more short walking trails could be carefully selected and developed close to the public road. The inclusion of historic buildings and scenic highlights such as waterfalls would draw the visitor onto these short paths, in the same way that they are now attracted to Torc Waterfall.

Visitors who are prepared for them could also be directed to the more rewarding and challenging experiences offered by the wilder areas of the national park. However, it is here that the challenge of managing a national park becomes clearly focused. Because of the wet climate and waterlogged soil, and because of the slow growing nature of much of the mountain and woodland vegetation, even relatively small numbers of visitors on a regular basis may cause significant damage. For instance, if visitors regularly follow a certain route in the mountains, the vegetation is quickly broken up underfoot and the wet peaty soil becomes churned into a swampy mess, in which walkers sink up to their ankles. Soon the walkers seek to bypass the worst stretches and more boggy ruts are formed parallel to the original route. Such damage will self-perpetuate until something is done. If significant numbers of visitors are discouraged or prevented from experiencing the natural zone of the park even in the most undamaging way possible – by walking – the park is surely failing to fulfil its second main objective, namely to enable people to visit and appreciate it.

There is a clear three-way choice: either visitors can be deliberately discouraged or prevented from walking in the wilder parts of the park, or an increasing rate of unsightly habitat damage and increasingly unsatisfactory walking conditions can be accepted, or a system of carefully constructed narrow and inconspicuous walking trails can be provided through representative areas of the park. It seems to me that walking trails are the appropriate option to take. Luckily, in Killarney National Park, taking the trails option is made somewhat easier by the fact that an extensive network of old tracks, 'green roads' and narrow paths have been in existence since the last century or earlier. Many of these are virtually forgotten and unused. Not only were they constructed skilfully by hand, and therefore fit with 'the lie' of the landscape rather than 'bulldozing' through it, they also have had over 150 years to 'settle' into the landscape and be obscured by the natural vegetation. This old network gives access to a rich variety of natural and historic features in areas of largely unspoiled wildness, pristine environment and great scenic beauty. If repaired and restored with the appropriate sensitivity and skill, and interconnected with a relatively small amount of newly constructed path, this network of trails could become one of the finest features of the Irish national parks system. It would be appropriate for the park's custodians to devote to a walking trail network the same careful planning, expert and loving craftsmanship, constant maintenance, and substantial expenditure that they have applied to other precious features such as Muckross House and Ross Castle.

In the last few years park rangers, assisted by volunteers, have developed the 'Old Kenmare Road' in the national park as a walking trail. Much of this work, such as the construction of boardwalks over areas of bog, and the repair and construction of stone paths and culverts has involved painstaking, physically demanding and skilful hand work. In inaccessible areas materials have been transported by helicopter to avoid habitat damage by overland haulage. Careful planning is an essential part of this ongoing work. The emphasis has been on minimising impact, and in recent years the use of heavy machinery has been avoided except in cases of absolute necessity. The rangers and volunteers involved in this project are handling the essential soul of Killarney National Park – areas of unique beauty and wildness that have been left virtually untouched in modern times. The skills and experience developed by the personnel involved in this work are a valuable resource for the national park. Whether the human and financial resources will be made available to continue this work and to develop other trails in the national park remains to be seen.

A walking trail constructed by volunteers and park rangers. (Bill Quirke)

Boardwalk over bog constructed by park rangers and volunteers on the Old Kenmare Road walking route. (Bill Quirke)

Path constructed by park rangers and volunteers on the Old Kenmare Road walking route. The most appropriate way to appreciate the park is by walking. (Bill Quirke)

Path construction work in progress on the Old Kenmare Road walking route. (Paudie O'Leary)

To avoid habitat damage path construction material has been transported by helicopter. (Paudie O'Leary)

There is a view that access to natural areas by significant numbers of people will inevitably involve destruction. There are those who believe that precious wild places can only survive if they remain inaccessible and unknown. The weight of available evidence across the world is certainly in favour of these views. The opportunity exists in Killarney National Park to show that it can be otherwise – to show that national parks can work.

Chapter 13

REMEMBERING WHO WE ARE:
A PERSONAL VIEW OF KILLARNEY NATIONAL PARK

Pádraig O'Donoghue

'May the God of wonder be with you, delighting you with thunder and bird-song, sunrise and flowers; enchanting your senses, filling your heart': the old Irish blessing that means so much here in Killarney. In a book on the national park, let us not forget the simple . . . the obvious . . . , we are all touched by the beauty of Killarney. Now as we enter a new century, we are realising that we need nature for more than just scientific or aesthetic reasons and a new understanding and intimacy with the natural world is developing.

Creation shows herself here in such a variety of ways: the powerful mountains, the fresh clear streams flowing into deep lakes; the whole web of life that fills the lush green woodlands and the open wetlands. Listen to the cries of the falcon or watch the wild deer moving on the mountain slopes. All of nature combines here to leave us in wonder and in awe.

In a world where 'wasting' time is considered almost a social ill, we who are privileged to visit the park are happy to 'waste' time sitting, walking or dreaming. I can touch boulders that were carved by the Ice Age or walk through woodlands where the Fianna hunted deer in ancient mythology. The yew trees, sacred to the druids, still grow here clinging mysteriously to life on bare rocks. Out in Lough Leane an island abbey reminds me of my Christian tradition and Killarney's own name has come from a sloe tree heavy laden with fruit. All around me my heritage is bound to the ways of the natural world.

Yet now in so many ways we have lost touch with nature and so too with ourselves. Our way of life makes us do things that directly or indirectly destroy the earth. Thomas Berry in his book, *The Dream of the Earth*, says 'our human destiny is integral with the destiny of the earth'. The reality of this statement is being felt all over the globe at present and whether it is the genuine concern we have over the food we give our children or the disgust at seeing the loss of natural habitat for development – we are becoming aware of the emptiness of our ways.

Surrounded by such progress stands the national park. When I look at the high mountains and wooded valleys shrouded in mist, I am coaxed into looking at the world in a different light. It is here I find healing; it is here I re-discover the lost meaning of reverence. Here I must trust my instincts again, my very own nature. I am challenged to let go of all the scientific facts and allow the mystery of it all to silence my anxious questioning. The beauty before me is enough. This experience of nature, this experience of being re-vitalised is our common heritage. Deep in my heart is the realisation, too, that I am an integral part of this web of life and not a separate entity. Even for my very existence I am totally reliant on so many natural occurrences; the air to breathe, the rain for water, the spring for germination of seeds that grow into vegetables and all the nourishing energy flowing from the distant sun. So much of nature taken for granted but so vital to our lives.

We can allow this experience, this awakening within ourselves to slip away. We can leave it behind when we leave the park. We have been conditioned into allowing this to happen. Is this contentment we experience, this beautiful completeness to be just for a few days or weeks? The holidays? Does it have to be this way? Must we go on living lives based on what we have instead of what we are? Must we relentlessly trample the earth and poison it with our wastes? Must we use percentages and terms like Gross National Product as standards for the quality of our lives? Could the failing of our major economic and social systems be that they are profit and production orientated instead of being centred on people and the earth?

Our modern world is faced with many problems as we see the collapse of what we take for granted. I do not know where it will all lead to, but I find great hope in the balance of nature, the cycle of the seasons, the eternal surprise of daffodils after the long dark winter. It is a wonderful time to be alive with so much change and searching going on. I know that some day, alive with the blessing of wonder, we will remember who we are and find our place within the unfolding story of the earth.

The Contributors

Bill Quirke studied Zoology at University College Dublin and carried out post graduate research on the ecology of Lough Leane in Killarney National Park. From 1982 to 1991 he worked full time as a contract ecologist in Killarney National Park. His work for the park included ecological monitoring of the Killarney Lakes; setting up the park field education centre at Knockreer House in 1987, initiating and running a park field education programme between 1987 and 1991. In 1981 he initiated the voluntary rhododendron clearance workcamps in the oakwoods of the park which led to the establishment of Groundwork – Irish Conservation Volunteers. He served as Groundwork's project leader in Killarney from 1981 to 1992. He initiated and was a co-founder of the Killarney Nature Conservation Group in 1985 and remained a member of that group until 1995. He now runs an ecological and environmental consultancy business with his wife Helena Twomey.

Richard Bradshaw studied botany at the University of Cambridge, England. He worked briefly in the USA and Scotland before accepting a lectureship in botany at Trinity College, Dublin, Ireland. In 1998, he moved to a forest research position in Sweden, and in 1996 he was appointed head of the research department of Environmental History and Climate at the Danish Ministry of the Environment. His research has focused on long-term forest ecosystem dynamics, and understanding the driving forces behind changes in forest composition. This has involved assessment of the interacting roles of climate change, human impact and disturbance of various origins particularly fire and grazing animals.

Terry Carruthers was born in Dublin, educated at St Vincents CBS, Dublin, and Birkbeck College, London. He was employed for 17 years as a ranger in Killarney National Park, where his special interest was the ecology of woodland birds and the conservation of the Greenland White-fronted geese. He published a number of scientific papers on his work and co-authored Birds of the Killarney National Park (OPW 1993). He later went on to complete his major work 'Kerry: A Natural History' (The Collins Press 1998). In 1998 he took a career break from the National Parks Service to develop his own company offering walking and wildlife holidays throughout Ireland and England. His principal interests are ornithology, walking, archaeology and travel.

Peter Coxon graduated with a BSc. degree in Biology and Geography from Sussex University in 1976 and subsequently went to Cambridge University to study for a PhD in the Sub-Department of Quaternary Research in the Botany Department. He gained his PhD (on Pleistocene environmental history of East Anglia) in 1979 and came to Trinity College Dublin that year where he has been in the Geography Department ever since. He is a Fellow of Trinity College and a Senior Lecturer in Geography and has carried out extensive research on the landscape history and palaeoenvironmental reconstruction of Ireland. He has also carried out geomorphological research in the western USA and in the Himalaya of Ladakh and Himachal Pradesh in northern India. A comprehensive list of his work is available on the WWW at: http://www2.tcd.ie/Geography/gg_res.html.

Alan Craig has a deep affection for Killarney National Park, derived from almost thirty years working involvement with this special place. He was the first biologist appointed, in 1971, to the staff of what was then the parks section of the Office of Public works, after studying botany and ecology at Trinity College Dublin and the University of Minnesota. Research for a Ph.D. on Irish late-glacial environmental history gave him a long-term view of ecological issues. Having been Chief Parks Superintendent for a few years, he is currently Director, Science and Habitats, with the National Parks and Wildlife division of Dúchas, the Heritage Service.

Daniel L. Kelly was born in Dublin, April 1948. An early introduction to plant lore through gardening was gradually overtaken by an interest in wild flowers, and from there to natural history in general. Took degree in Botany at Trinity College, University of Dublin. Introduced to the Killarney woods by Professor William A. Watts, who supervised his undergraduate thesis on the Muckross woods, and subsequently his Ph.D. thesis on Irish native woodlands. After four years in the West Indies, returned to Trinity college as a lecturer in Botany. His research interests now oscillate between Irish woodlands and tropical forests. His loyalty to the Killarney woods is undimmed, and he continues to find fresh delight exploring and studying them.

Bairbre Ní Fhloinn is a collector and archivist with the Department of Irish folklore in University College Dublin. Her collecting work has taken her to many parts of Ireland, and she has also studied folklore at the University of Helsinki in Finland, and more recently in the University of Cagliari in Sardinia.

She has done extensive research on the luck-beliefs of fishermen in the past and present, and she has just completed a book on the subject which is due for publication shortly by Comhairle Bhealoideas Éireann.

William O'Brien is an archaeology graduate of University College Cork where he completed doctoral research in 1987 on the subject of ancient copper mining in Ireland. His research interests lie in Bronze Age studies, with particular reference to early metallurgy, and the prehistory of south-west Ireland. He is director of the Ross Island project which is presently investigating the mining heritage of the Killarney area. He lectures on prehistory in the Department of Archaeology, National University of Ireland, Galway.

Pádraig O'Donoghue is from Killarney. He has a great love of Kerry's varied landscapes and with Fiona his wife is committed to developing a sustainable lifestyle. His interests include hillwalking and canoeing, photography and gardening. He works both as an arts instructor and as a community facilitator. Of particular interest to him are the links between ecology and spirituality and he regularly gives workshops throughout the country dealing with these topics.

Grellan Rourke studied Architecture at University College Dublin and subsequently followed post-graduate studies in Architectural and Building conservation in Belgium and Italy. He is a Senior Conservation Architect with Dúchas – The Heritage Service and has been working in their National Monuments Section for 21 years. He is a founder-director of the Institute for the Conservation of Historic and Artistic Works in Ireland (ICHAWI) and is an executive member of the Irish committee of I.C.O.M.O.S. He is a joint author of *The Forgotten Hermitage of Skellig Michael* and a forthcoming publication on High Island, Co. Galway.

Seán Ryan has continued to walk the mountains of Kerry and study and photograph the red deer of Killarney since the mid-fifties. He has previously contributed descriptive chapters on Irish mountains in *Wild Ireland*, and *The Book of the Irish Countryside*. His recently published book, *The Wild Red Deer of Killarney*, has received wide acclaim. A retired accountant, he is at present studying for a PhD in history at The National University of Ireland, Cork.

Richard Thorn graduated from Trinity College Dublin in 1978 with a degree in Natural Sciences (in Physical Geography). He was awarded a PhD in 1984 for work on the leaching of nitrate from soil to groundwater. He worked in the private sector in the area of site investigation and held lecturing positions in TCD and DIT before being appointed as a lecturer in Sligo Institute of Technology in 1982. While in Sligo he worked on degree, masters and PhD programmes in environmental science and had a particular interest in the area of karst landscapes and groundwater pollution. He held the post of Head of the Department of Environmental Science in Sligo before being appointed in 1994 as Head of the Castlebar Campus of the Galway-Mayo Institute of Technology.

Index

Entries in bold type indicate illustrations